Study Guide

to accompany

Understanding American Government

SIXTH EDITION

Rogers • Bresler • Friedrich
Karlesky • Stephenson, Jr. • Turner

Study Guide to accompany Rogers, Bresler, Friedrich, Karlesky, Stephenson, Jr. and Turner's UNDERSTANDING AMERICAN GOVERNMENT, 6th edition

ISBN: 978-1-61882-886-6

Contents

Introduction

CHAPTER REVIEW

Learning Objectives

After studying the Introduction you should be able to:

1. Define politics and explain how economic and ideological differences result in political conflict.

2. Explain the purpose of government.

3. Understand the values and goals of democracy, how they conflict, and what makes democracy work.

4. Comment on the changing role of politics and government in American life and how government is so particularly pervasive today.

Chapter Outline and Summary

I. Introduction

    A. The purpose of this text is to explain the importance of politics and government and how it affects our lives.

II. What is Politics?

    A. Introduction

        1. Although considered negatively by many, politics can be an honorable activity.
        2. Politics is about ways to resolve differences without resorting to violence.
        3. The differences between the desires and values of groups are at the root of the political process.
        4. Aristotle called politics the "master science" since he believed politics provided the means by which a community of people with differing views and interests could strive for collective survival and advancement.

B. Politics and Economics

    1. Groups and individuals compete over limited economic resources and government policies affecting them.

    2. In the American form of capitalism, government complements, coexists, and regulates an economy that is largely in private hands.

C. Politics and Ideas

    1. Ideology refers to the kind of government people think they should have and what it should do.

    2. Ideological differences spark political controversies that politicians attempt to mediate.

III. Why Government?

A. Introduction

    1. Government is the set of organizations within which much of the political process takes place.

B. To Establish Justice, Insure Domestic Tranquility, and Secure the Blessings of Liberty

    1. Government is needed to establish justice, domestic tranquility, and secure liberty.

C. To Provide for the Common Defense

    1. Government is needed to provide for the common defense of the nation.

D. To Promote the General Welfare

    1. Government is needed to promote the general welfare of its citizens.

       a. Should government be active and strive for a positive state, or be more passive and opt for a minimalist state?

IV. What Is Democracy?

A. Democratic Values and Goals

    1. Democracy requires a system of government based on majority rule, minority rights, individual rights, and equality.

    2. These four objectives may be in conflict with each other, with different political systems balancing them differently.

    3. American democracy involves constitutionalism, the principle of limiting governmental power by a written constitution.

B. Making Democracy Work

    1. In order for democracy to function, the people and leaders must accept compromise, accept democratic values and goals, and support the process by which agreement is reached.

V. Why Do Politics and Government Matter?

    A. Government played a small role in the early days of the American Republic.

    B. Today the national government pervades society, the economy, and individual citizens' lives.

VI. Summary

Key Terms, Concepts, and Personalities

After studying the Introduction you should be able to identify and describe the significance of:

capitalism	minimalist state
collective goods	politics
democracy	positive state
government	power
ideology	

TESTING YOUR UNDERSTANDING

Completion

1. The best-known and most straightforward definition of politics is the study of "who gets _____, _____, and _____."

2. An economic system based upon private ownership and free economic competition is called _____.

3. _____ is a set of ideas concerning the proper political and economic system under which people should live.

4. _____ _____ are available for the benefit of all citizens, whether they paid taxes for them or not.

5. In order for a democracy to function effectively, the people and their leaders must be willing to accept _____.

6. _____ is the ability to get someone to act in accordance with your wishes.

Compare and Contrast

1. politics, economics, and ideology

2. politics and government

3. positive state and minimalist state

4. majority rule, minority rights, individual rights, and equality

True-False

1. Politics is the process of peacefully reconciling social and economic differences.   T   F

2. The Civil War illustrates the importance of politics as a means to resolve differences without violence.   T   F

3. Economic liberty is considered an absolute right in the American system.   T   F

4. Even in the early days of the American Republic, people were making great demands on the national government.   T   F

5. Politics is a process and government is the set of organizations within which much of that process takes place.   T   F

Multiple Choice

1. Aristotle called politics the "master science" because:
   a. it can explain all the mysteries of human life and nature.
   b. it provides a means for people to strive for collective survival and advancement.
   c. involves relationships between people rather than animals or inanimate objects.
   d. it is the constant that pervades all other sciences.

2. Which of the following statements about politics and economics is false?
   a. The national government spends well over $3 trillion annually.
   b. When economic self-interest is at stake, most people press for programs that serve their self-interests.
   c. Until the presidency of Franklin D. Roosevelt, America practiced a form of pure capitalism.
   d. Historically, economic and political power in the United States have been divided.

3. Which of the following statements about politics and ideas is true?
   a. Ideology is about political ideas and does not include ideas about the economic system.
   b. Ideological differences among Americans spark many political controversies.
   c. Ideological debates are only about relations with other countries.
   d. Money usually represents the source of compromise in ideological differences between people.

4. Without government, life would be "solitary, poor, nasty, brutish, and short" is a statement attributed to:
   a. Oliver Wendell Holmes.   c. Thomas Hobbes.
   b. John Locke.   d. Ronald Reagan.

5. Government enterprises such as dam construction, wilderness protection, and providing for the needy are examples of:
   a. the minimalist state.   c. interest group policies.
   b. social welfare policies.   d. collective goods.

6. Each of the following is a precept of democracy except:
   a. economic equality.   c. full protection of minority rights.
   b. majority rule.   d. protection of individual rights.

7. Which of the following statements about democratic values and goals is false?
   a. Minority rights limit the kind of laws majorities can pass.
   b. Efforts to achieve equality may involve restraints on individual liberty.
   c. Different political systems balance the four democratic values differently.
   d. Equality before the law guarantees everyone the same influence in public affairs.

8. In order for a democracy to work:
   a. the leaders must accept the principles of a positivist state.
   b. the government must have a written constitution.
   c. the people and leaders must be willing to accept compromise.
   d. economic equality must be reached.

9. In the early days of the American Republic:
   a. Washington was the only true cosmopolitan city in the country.
   b. people expected little from the national government.
   c. foreign affairs were of particular importance.
   d. Congress met more frequently than they do today.

10. Democracy is based on:
    a. majority rule.
    b. minority rights.
    c. individual rights.
    d. equality before the law.
    e. all of the above

Essay

1. Answer the question posed in the text, "What is politics?" Write your own definition of politics and defend your definition by citing examples from everyday life and current events.

2. Explain how political and economic issues are often related in American society.

3. What does the Preamble to the Constitution of the United States tell us about the purpose of government?

4. Discuss the four precepts of democracy and explain how they may be in conflict with each other.

5. How has the role of government changed from the early days of the American Republic? Give examples.

Research Topics and Practical Applications

1. Using newspapers and/or weekly news magazines, find current events that illustrate conflicts involving the four precepts of democracy (majority rule, minority rights, individual liberty, and equality). Make a list of the examples you found and categorize them according to which precepts of democracy are involved. Try to determine what caused each conflict, whether a fair political compromise was reached, and how the compromise was reached. What do your findings tell us about the democratic political process?

2. Knowing what you do about the role of the national government in the early days of the American Republic and the role of the national government today, write a scenario of what the role of the national government might be one to two hundred years from now. Use the discussion in the last section of Chapter 1 ("Why do Politics and Government Matter?") as a guide to your scenario. Discuss how the government might be involved in the economy and everyday life. In writing your scenario, assume that the democratic process and the principles of democracy will be preserved in the future.

ANSWER KEY

Completion

1. what, when, how
2. capitalism
3. Ideology
4. Collective goods
5. compromise
6. Power

True-False

1. T
2. T
3. F
4. F
5. T

Multiple Choice

1. b
2. c
3. b
4. c
5. d
6. a
7. d
8. c
9. b
10. e

Chapter 1

THE CONSTITUTION OF THE UNITED STATES

CHAPTER REVIEW

Learning Objectives

After studying Chapter 1 you should be able to:

1. Explain the nature and functions of a constitution.

2. Understand the theoretical underpinnings of the Declaration of Independence.

3. Evaluate the strengths and weaknesses of the Articles of Confederation.

4. Summarize the history of the constitutional convention, including backgrounds of the framers, procedures, and compromises reached.

5. Describe the struggle for ratification and how the Bill of Rights fits into this struggle.

6. Understand and define the major features of the Constitution, including secularism, republicanism, checks and balances, federalism, the Electoral College, and adaptability.

7. Explain how the Constitution can be changed both formally by amendment and informally.

8. Discuss the importance of judicial review as originating in *Marbury v. Madison*.

Chapter Outline and Summary

I.   Introduction

    A. The U.S. Constitution is the Basis for the American Political System

II. What Is a Constitution?

    A. Constitutionalism

        1. Constitutionalism is the belief of limiting power by written charter.

        2. Constitutions take different forms in different countries.

        3. Constitutions embody intangibles that enable them to work and survive.

    B. Constitutional Functions

        1. A constitution outlines the organization of government.

        2. A constitution grants power and authority to government.

        3. A constitution can outline the basic rights of citizens.

        4. A constitution may serve as a symbol of the country.

III. The Road to Nationhood

    A. The Declaration of Independence: The Idea of Consent

        1. Between 1763 and 1776 British attempts at direct control clashed with colonial self-interest and identity.

        2. The Declaration of Independence stated colonists' grievances against British rule.

        3. The Declaration also expressed the political ideas and values of the day including the following themes:

            a. Humankind shares an equality: life, liberty, and the pursuit of happiness.

            b. Government is the creation and servant of the people.

            c. The rights that all people intrinsically possess constitute a higher law binding government.

            d. Governments are bound by their own laws.

    B. The Articles of Confederation: The Idea of Compact

        1. State autonomy was preserved and the states maintained power.

        2. Equal representation for the states was preserved.

        3. The central government was granted only a few important powers.

        4. There was no separate executive or national courts.

5. Amendments were almost impossible since unanimous consent from all the states was required.

IV. The Making of the Constitution

    A. Prelude to Philadelphia

        1. The major deficiencies of the Articles were a weak central government and too much power in state governments.

        2. Shays' Rebellion illustrated the economic problems and weaknesses of the central government.

        3. The Annapolis Convention led to a call for a constitutional convention.

        4. One notable success of the Articles was the Northwest Ordinance, laying the basis for government of lands in the West.

    B. The Philadelphia Convention

        1. America of 1787 was sparsely populated, weakly defended, and internationally isolated.

        2. The delegates to the convention were among the most notable and talented of their day.

        3. Procedures and compromises at the convention:

            a. Deliberations were held in secret.

            b. The Great Compromise (Connecticut Plan) took the Virginia Plan for a strong national government and the New Jersey Plan for strong state governments and created numerical representation in the lower house and equal state representation in the upper house.

            c. The three-fifths compromise allowed slaves to be counted as a fraction for representation purposes.

            d. Ironically, a majority of Americans (slaves and women) were denied representation and participation.

    C. Ratification

        1. Article 7 required the approval of nine state conventions.

        2. Supporters of the Constitution called themselves Federalists and the other side Antifederalists.

        3. *The Federalist Papers*, a collection of essays supporting the Constitution, is a major source of American political theory.

        4. Antifederalists believed the Constitution was conceived illegally, weakened state governments, threatened individual liberty, and promoted a commercial empire.

V. Features of the Constitution

    A. Republicanism, Divided Powers, and Federalism

        1. Republican government (i.e., representatives elected by the people) is one of divided powers.

        2. A mixture of democratic/nondemocratic elements include popular elections, indirect popular elections, and appointment.

        3. The Constitution limited government and diffused and dispersed power in order to prevent Madison's fear of tyranny.

        4. Power was divided horizontally in a system of checks and balances where the legislative, executive, and judicial branches share power.

        5. Federalism divided power vertically between national and state governments.

        6. Side effects of these attempts to check tyranny:

            a. It sometimes has been more difficult to deal with threats to individual liberty in the states.

            b. Fragmented powers have sometimes made it hard to govern.

    B. A Single and Independent Executive

        1. Executive authority was suspect at the time of the Convention.

        2. The Electoral College was a compromise between electing the president by the people, Congress, or state legislatures.

    C. Adaptability

        1. Although a product of the eighteenth century, the Constitution has adapted over time.

        2. The Constitution's brevity necessitates interpretation.

        3. There is elasticity in the language of the Constitution.

            a. Some words and phrases have no precise meaning.

            b. The elastic clause gives Congress implied powers that have been used to meet new challenges and needs.

        4. The Constitution exalts procedure over substance, thus avoiding time-related policy choices.

D. Amending the Constitution

    1. Amendment by the Rules

        a. The Constitution has been amended relatively few times—27 times in over 200 years.

        b. Amendments may be proposed by Congress or state legislatures.

            1. Either by a two-thirds vote in the House and Senate (only method used thus far).

            2. Or by a national convention convened by Congress upon petition by two-thirds of the states (never used).

        c. Amendments must be ratified by the states.

            1. Either by three-fourths of the state legislatures (used 26 times).

            2. Or, by conventions in three-fourths of the states (used once).

    2. Change by Custom and Evolution

        a. Changing values, expectations, and conditions have influenced constitutional attitudes and practices.

        b. Examples include requirements for representatives to live in their districts, political parties, and presidential electors' pledge to support their party's ticket.

VI. Judicial Review Comes to the Supreme Court

A. *Marbury v. Madison:* The Case of the Undelivered Commissions

    1. After the 1800 election, the Federalist Congress authorized 42 new justices of the peace but some of these appointments were not delivered before the new president (Jefferson) took office.

    2. William Marbury asked the Supreme Court to force delivery through a writ of mandamus.

    3. Chief Justice Marshall decided that Marbury should have his job, that the Supreme Court can rule on the legality of actions of the executive, but that the Court could not issue a writ of mandamus because it was not in their original jurisdiction.

B. The Significance of *Marbury*

    1. Officers of the government were bound by law.

    2. Laws contrary to the Constitution were not valid.

    3. The Court claimed authority to decide what the Constitution means (judicial review).

    4. The Court rejected the states' desire to interpret the Constitution as argued in the Kentucky and Virginia Resolutions.

C. Judicial Review and the Framers

    1. Some framers expected the Court to exercise judicial review.

    2. Much controversy stems from the fact that the Constitution says nothing about how its words are to be interpreted. (See "Politics and Ideas: Whose Constitution Is It?")

    3. Marshall saw judicial review as only a modest power.

VII. Summary

Key Terms, Concepts, and Personalities

After studying Chapter 1 you should be able to identify and describe the significance of:

Annapolis Convention	Articles of Confederation
Antifederalists	checks and balances
constitutionalism	New Jersey Plan
elastic clause	Northwest Ordinance
The Federalist Papers	republican (or representative) government
Federalists	Shays' Rebellion
Great Compromise	three-fifths compromise
judicial review	Virginia Plan
Kentucky and Virginia Resolutions	writ of mandamus
Marbury v. Madison	

TESTING YOUR UNDERSTANDING

Completion

1. The belief in limiting governmental power by a written charter is called _____.

2. The Declaration of Independence contains a strong belief that government is the creation and servant of the _____.

3. Under the Articles of Confederation the _____ retained most political power.

4. The _____ solved the problem of how to count slaves for purposes of congressional representation.

5. Supporters of the proposed Constitution called themselves _____.

6. Direct election of the president by the people, Congress, or state legislatures was avoided by creation of the _____ _____.

7. The _____ _____ authorizes Congress to pass laws allowing it to carry into execution its expressed powers.

8. John Marshall could not help William Marbury get his judicial appointment because the writ of mandamus he requested was not part of the Court's _____ jurisdiction.

Compare and Contrast

1. Shays' Rebellion and Annapolis Convention

2. Virginia Plan, New Jersey Plan, and Great Compromise

3. Federalists and Antifederalists

4. ratification of the Constitution and the Bill of Rights

5. separation of powers and federalism

6. *Marbury v. Madison* and judicial review

7. original jurisdiction and appellate jurisdiction

True-False

1. The British Constitution can be changed by an act of Parliament. T F

2. Virtual unanimity existed in the colonies in favor of declaring independence in 1776. T F

3. The Articles of Confederation provided for no separate executive and no national courts. T F

4. One of the few successes of Congress under the Articles of Confederation was the Northwest Ordinance. T F

5. Under the original Constitution, a majority of Americans were denied representation and participation. T F

6. As written, the Constitution facilitates the creation of political parties and interest groups, called factions by Madison. T F

7. The Constitution of the United States is longer than most state constitutions. T F

Multiple Choice

1. All of the following are constitutional functions *except*:
   a. providing an outline for the organization of government.
   b. establishing a formal economic system for the country.
   c. granting power to governmental institutions.
   d. serving as a symbol of the nation.

2. Prior to the American Revolution, British leaders in London:
   a. attempted to force the colonies to raise armies for self defense.
   b. repealed the Townsend Acts, allowing the colonies to tax.
   c. gave the colonies power to appoint their own governors.
   d. attempted to bring the colonies under more direct control.

3. Which of the following is not a major theme of the Declaration of Independence?
   a. Humankind shares an equality.
   b. Government is a divinely ordained compact between people and God.
   c. The rights that all people intrinsically possess constitute a higher law binding government.
   d. Governments are bound by their own laws.

4. One of the main provisions of the Articles of Confederation was that:
   a. it guaranteed equal representation for the states.
   b. it established a weak separate executive department.
   c. the national courts were given only limited appellate jurisdiction.
   d. amendments could only be made with the approval of Congress and a majority of state legislatures.

5. One of the major deficiencies of the Articles of Confederation was:
   a. too great a policymaking role for the national courts.
   b. the ability of the states to declare war separately.
   c. the ease by which the Articles could be amended by the states.
   d. the absence of sufficient power in the central government.

6. The 1786 Annapolis Convention was originally promoted as a means of:
   a. consolidating the American military forces.
   b. creating a uniform tariff policy toward Britain.
   c. improving commercial relations among the states.
   d. writing a new national constitution.

7. One of the few successes of the Articles of Confederation was the:
   a. Annapolis Convention.
   b. Northwest Ordinance.
   c. Townsend Acts.
   d. three-fifths compromise.

8. The framers of the Constitution:
   a. were among the most talented and intellectual people of the day.
   b. were mostly farmers.
   c. represented a reassembling of the generation that had set the Revolution in motion.
   d. were all committed to writing a completely new Constitution.

9. In order for the new Constitution to go into effect it had to be approved by:
   a. all of the state legislatures.
   b. seven of the thirteen state legislatures.
   c. popularly elected conventions in nine states.
   d. popularly elected conventions in all of the states.

10. Antifederalists opposed the Constitution because it:
    a. was conceived in an illegal manner.
    b. seemed designed to promote a commercial empire.
    c. failed to include a bill of rights.
    d. all of the above

11. The constitutional arrangement where power is divided and shared horizontally is called:
    a. republicanism.
    b. popularism.
    c. separation of powers.
    d. federalism.

12. The Constitution requires amendments to be:
    a. initiated by Congress.
    b. initiated by the President.
    c. approved by two-thirds of the state legislatures.
    d. approved by three-fourths of the states.

13. In *Marbury v. Madison*, Chief Justice John Marshall ruled that:
    a. a writ of mandamus was an improper constitutional remedy.
    b. the Supreme Court did not possess original jurisdiction.
    c. the Court could not rule on the legality of presidential action.
    d. Marbury would receive his judicial appointment.

14. The significance of *Marbury v. Madison* was that:
    a. officers of the government could be called to account in court.
    b. statutes contrary to the Constitution were not valid.
    c. the Court claimed authority to decide what the Constitution means.
    d. all of the above

15. The Kentucky and Virginia Resolutions of 1798:
    a. called for the Supreme Court to have the power of judicial review.
    b. favored decentralized over centralized judicial review.
    c. claimed for the states the final authority to interpret the Constitution.
    d. called for Congress to have the power of judicial review.

16. Judicial review:
    a. was favored by a majority of the founding fathers.
    b. was favorably argued in *The Federalist* papers.
    c. can be found in Article III of the Constitution.
    d. was not mentioned in the state ratifying conventions.

Essay

1. Explain what is meant by "constitutionalism" and delineate the major functions of a constitution.

2. What happened at the Philadelphia Convention? How would you characterize the delegates to the convention? Describe the compromises reached at the convention.

3. Explain how the Constitution diffuses and disperses power. What unpleasant side effects might occur as a result of this arrangement?

4. Explain how the Constitution is changed, both formally (by amendments) and informally (by custom and evolution). Give examples of each. How does the process of amending the U.S. Constitution differ from amending the state constitutions?

5. What was the significance of *Marbury v. Madison?* Evaluate judicial review in terms of democracy.

Research Topics and Practical Applications

1. Find a copy of the constitution of a country other than the United States. Answer the following questions regarding the constitution you chose, comparing your answer with characteristics of the American Constitution:
   a. How is the government organized and what are the major branches of government?
   b. How is power horizontally divided between the branches of government?
   c. Is there a vertical division of government (federal or confederal)? How is power divided vertically?
   d. Does the constitution provide for elections of government officials? If so, what is the nature of these elections and are political parties mentioned?
   e. Is there a bill of rights in the constitution? What is the extent of these rights and what limitations are placed on them?
   f. Is judicial review mentioned? If so, what is the procedure for judicial review?
   g. What is the procedure for amending the constitution? Does it appear to be easy or difficult to amend the constitution?

2. Examine how the Constitution has withstood the test of time. Is it truly an adaptable document? What aspects of it might you consider outdated? Give examples and reasons why. Examine a contemporary issue, such as abortion, the environment, nuclear power, or high-tech communications. How might these become constitutional issues? Can the Constitution fairly deal with issues such as these that the founding fathers could never have foreseen?

ANSWER KEY

Completion

1. constitutionalism
2. people
3. states
4. three-fifths compromise
5. Federalists
6. Electoral College
7. elastic clause
8. original

True-False

1. T
2. F
3. T
4. T
5. T
6. T
7. F

Multiple Choice

1. b
2. d
3. b
4. a
5. d
6. c
7. b
8. a
9. c
10. d
11. c
12. d
13. a
14. d
15. c
16. b

Chapter 2

FEDERALISM: STATES IN THE UNION

CHAPTER REVIEW

Learning Objectives

After studying Chapter 2 you should be able to:

1. Understand the idea of federalism and differentiate it from confederate and unitary forms of government.

2. Explain the historical role of the states in the American constitutional system as it relates to the national government.

3. Compare and contrast the legal, fiscal, and political relationships among levels of government in the United States.

4. Explain why the national government and state and local governments conflict or cooperate over matters of public policy.

Chapter Outline and Summary

I. Introduction

   A. The principal characteristic of a federal system is the sharing of power.

   B. Federalism is a complex, adaptable system of relationships in which states have begun to assume a more energetic and vigorous role in domestic policy.

   C. Common things such as drivers tests, marriage licenses, tax returns, and public schooling, illustrate the crucial role of state governments.

II. The Idea of Federalism

    A. Introduction

        1. Federalism is a system of government in which a national and state governments share power within the same political system.

        2. Both national and state governments have jurisdiction over individuals in a federal system.

        3. The federal system is a compromise between a strong central government and a league of separate states.

    B. Confederate and Unitary Forms of Government

        1. A confederation is a loose collection of states in which principal power lies at the level of the individual state rather than at the level of the central or national government.

            a. Confederations are founded on the political idea of diversity and local control, allowing states to pursue diverse approaches to policy.

            b. Historically, the United States under the Articles of Confederation is an example of a confederation.

        2. A unitary system of government is one in which principal power within the political system lies at the level of a national or central government rather than at the level of a smaller unit.

            a. Unitary structures rest on the value of unity and assume that there is a national interest in meeting needs and problems in a particular way.

            b. The government of France and each of the 50 American states are unitary systems.

    C. Unity and Diversity in the Federal System

        1. States differ in many ways such as size, economy, resources, and population.

        2. To what degree should these differences allow diverse public policies, and when should national policies prevail?

    D. A Comparative Perspective on Federalism

        1. Several diverse countries in the world have federal constitutional systems.

        2. Common to all federal systems is the attempt to pull together disparate groups (based on culture, language, geography, or religion) while acknowledging their separate identities.

        3. The relative power of the central government and constituent groups varies among federal systems.

4. Some of the world's great political conflicts stem from the struggle to define the balance between national purposes and group needs in a federal system. French-speaking Quebec in Canada and the former Soviet republics are two examples.

III. States in the Constitutional System

A. Introduction

1. The 50 American states are integral parts of our social and political consciousness and play a crucial role in the American political system. For example, they administer social welfare policies, amend the Constitution, and shape electoral contests.

B. The Rise of the National Government

1. The conflict between unity and diversity also shaped the relationship between the national and state governments in the early years.

2. Cooperation and conflict occurred, which ultimately was tested in war.

3. The end of the Civil War marked the beginning of rapid change.

4. The role of the national government increased after the Great Depression and after World War II.

C. Expressed and Implied Powers

1. Expressed powers are specifically enumerated as belonging to Congress and the president. Examples include the power to regulate interstate commerce, coin money, and declare war.

2. Implied powers permit Congress to make laws that are "necessary and proper" to execute the expressed powers.

   a. *McCulloch v. Maryland* (1819) first interpreted the "necessary and proper" clause to allow implied powers to the national government.

   b. *McCulloch* also reaffirmed the principle of national supremacy.

D. Reserved Powers: What Do the States Do?

1. According to the Tenth Amendment powers not delegated to the United States, nor prohibited to the states, are reserved to the states.

2. Among powers reserved for the states are "police" responsibilities for the health, safety, and welfare of citizens, such as:

   a. Responsibility for preventing and prosecuting criminal activities.

   b. Regulating a variety of matters having to do with public safety, business, and commerce.

   c. Providing for the universal education of its citizens.

E. Local Government: A Political Landscape of Contrasts

   1. One of the reserved powers of the states is control over the structure and powers of local governments.

      a. In the late nineteenth century many local governments were granted home rule, which is the power to determine (within limits) their powers and functions.

      b. Traditionally, local governments only have the power that is given to them by the state (Dillon's Rule).

   2. Although local governments are primarily concerned with the unglamorous services essential to civilized life, occasionally their decisions cause a local crisis or controversy, invoking intense citizen interest.

IV. Government Relationships in the Federal System

   A. Models of Federalism

      1. Dual federalism posits the view that national and state governments are separate and independent from each other, with each level exercising its own powers in its own jurisdiction.

      2. Cooperative federalism posits the view that across a wide range of public policies, despite occasional conflict, all levels of government are intertwined and work closely with one another.

   B. Legal Relationships

      1. The Supreme Court has played a major role in settling conflicts between different levels of government.

      2. The Court has generally supported the national government and national constitutional values in resolving conflicts with the states, particularly in the following areas:

         a. Regulation of interstate commerce.

         b. Interpretation of the due process clause of the Fourteenth Amendment.

         c. Interpretation of the equal protection clause of the Fourteenth Amendment.

   C. Fiscal Relationships

      1. A categorical grant-in-aid is a transfer of cash from the national government to state or local governments for some specific purpose.

      2. A block grant is a transfer of cash from the national to state and local governments for use in some broad policy area allowing greater discretion in its use.

D. Political Relationships

    1. Political relationships in the federal system may derive from local or state officeholders as a group making demands on the national government.

    2. Many of the political relationships in the federal system derive from differences among states and localities as they compete with each other to press their individual interests. Examples include:

        a. The long history of slavery and discrimination in the South.

        b. Environmental policy.

        c. Defense contracts.

V. Federalism in the Twenty-First Century

    A. The national government has become more dominant over the past two centuries.

    B. The states have recently become public policy innovators, particularly in the areas of education, welfare, and the environment.

    C. Although the states are doing more, the national government has cut funds and increased the number of regulations applying to state and local governments (unfunded mandates).

VI. Summary

Key Terms, Concepts, and Personalities

After studying Chapter 2 you should be able to identify and describe the significance of:

block grant	home rule
categorical grant-in-aid	implied powers
confederation	interstate compact
cooperative federalism	new federalism
delegated powers	reserved powers
Dillon's Rule	Sixteenth Amendment
dual federalism	Tenth Amendment
Electoral College	unfunded mandate
expressed powers	unitary system
federalism	

TESTING YOUR UNDERSTANDING

Completion

1. Federalism is the product and symbol of the continuing ideological struggle between the values of _____ and _____.

2. The 50 American states are themselves _____ governments because the principal power within each state lies with the state government.

3. _____ powers are specifically enumerated in the Constitution as belonging to Congress.

4. The Supreme Court case of _____ v. _____ interpreted the "necessary and proper" clause as allowing expansive power to the national government.

5. The power to administer public education is an example of a _____ power.

6. A model of federalism that views national and state governments as separate and independent from each other is called _____ _____.

7. The single most important characteristic of federalism in the twentieth century has become cooperative _____ _____.

8. The most predominant form of national aid to the states takes the form of _____ _____ - _____ - _____.

Compare and Contrast

1. confederate, unitary, and federal forms of government

2. concurrent, delegated, and reserved powers

3. expressed and implied powers

4. dual federalism and cooperative federalism

5. due process clause and equal protection clause

6. categorical grant-in-aid and block grant

True-False

1. The federal system is a compromise between a strong central government and a league of separate states. T F

2. A major fault of the Articles of Confederation was the absence of a central foreign and military policy. T F

3. States act in some measure as administrative units to carry out national social welfare programs. T F

4. *McCulloch v. Maryland* established the right of states to determine what is "necessary and proper" to carry out public policies. T F

5. Among the powers reserved for the states is the responsibility for preventing and prosecuting criminal activities. T F

6. Studies have shown that citizen interest in the affairs of local government is almost nonexistent. T F

7. Through a process of cooperative agreements, the states have the power to regulate interstate commerce. T F

Multiple Choice

1. Federalism is the product and symbol of the continuing ideological struggle between the values of:
   a. freedom and equality.
   b. unity and diversity.
   c. justice and protection.
   d. individualism and nationalism.

2. The government of France is a:
   a. confederate system.
   b. unitary system.
   c. federal system.
   d. decentralized system.

3. In creating a federal system, the most important consideration of the framers of the Constitution in the move to a national government were:
   a. economic policy.
   b. foreign policy.
   c. military policy.
   d. all of the above

4. Federal systems are found in:
   a. France.
   b. Britain.
   c. United States.
   d. all of the above

5. The example of Quebec province in Canada illustrates:
   a. political conflict in a federal system.
   b. a federal system based on religion.
   c. the disintegration of a federal system.
   d. none of the above

6. The states play a crucial role in all of the following activities except:
   a. administering social welfare policies.
   b. regulating interstate commerce.
   c. amending the Constitution.
   d. shaping electoral contests at the national level.

7. The number of electoral votes for each state is equal to the number of:
   a. counties in each state.
   b. voting-age citizens in each state.
   c. its members in the House of Representatives.
   d. its members in the House and Senate combined.

8. The Supreme Court case of *McCulloch v. Maryland* confirmed the national government's:
   a. delegated powers.
   b. expressed powers.
   c. implied powers.
   d. reserved powers.

9. The right of reserved powers was guaranteed in the:
   a. Tenth Amendment.
   b. Eighteenth Amendment.
   c. Twenty-first Amendment.
   d. Supreme Court case of *McCulloch v. Maryland*.

10. According to the text, the most visible and pervasive role of the state is in the area of:
    a. interstate commerce.
    b. education.
    c. health.
    d. business regulation.

11. Home rule:
    a. granted greater power to county governments.
    b. established the system of general purpose local governments.
    c. created a surge in the number of local governments.
    d. gave local governments the power, within limits, to determine their own powers and functions.

12. Dillon's Rule:
    a. measures the difference between dual federalism and cooperative federalism powers.
    b. states that local governments only have the powers that are given to them by the state.
    c. considers local government to be superior to the state.
    d. considers the state government to be superior to the federal government.
    e. none of the above

13. When local law enforcement authorities call on the FBI to help them solve a crime, the kind of federalism illustrated is:
    a. dual federalism.
    b. layer cake federalism.
    c. cooperative federalism.
    d. chocolate cake federalism.

14. The ability of the national government to forbid sponsored prayers in public schools stems from the Supreme Court's interpretation of the:
    a. establishment clause.
    b. necessary and proper clause.
    c. interstate commerce clause.
    d. elastic clause.

15. Political conflicts between national and state and local governments derive from:
    a. scarce resources.
    b. the search for the balance between state and national power.
    c. the social and economic differences among the states.
    d. all of the above

Essay

1. Explain the differences between confederate, unitary, and federal forms of government. Illustrate the differences with examples.

2. Describe the various ways in which the states play a crucial role in the American political system.

3. Answer the question posed in the text, "What do the states do?" What policy areas are left primarily to the states?

4. In what ways is money "a kind of glue that binds the different levels of government?" Describe the historical evolution of fiscal relationships between the national, and state and local governments.

5. What are the bases for political competition between the states? Using examples, describe how this competition has created tension in the federal system.

Research Topics and Practical Application

1. Make a list of all the governmental units that have direct jurisdiction over your home town residence. Explain the ways in which you are affected by each governmental unit. Describe any controversies that have occurred between any of these governmental units in recent years. You may have to consult a local library for information on these.

2. The flip side of state and local competition for economic investment and development is the concept of NIMBY, or "not in my back yard." Investigate this phenomenon. Besides the storage of nuclear waste, what other projects might states and localities resist? Why might people not want a particular economic development project located nearby? Find examples of this phenomenon and document them according to the issues, individuals, and levels of government involved. What was the outcome of the examples you examined?

ANSWER KEY

Completion

1. unity and diversity
2. unitary
3. Expressed
4. *McCulloch v. Maryland*
5. reserved
6. dual federalism
7. fiscal relationships
8. categorical grants-in-aid

True-False

1. T
2. T
3. T
4. F
5. T
6. F
7. F

Multiple Choice

1. b
2. b
3. d
4. c
5. a
6. b
7. d
8. c
9. a
10. b
11. d
12. b
13. c
14. a
15. d

Chapter 3

CIVIL LIBERTIES AND CIVIL RIGHTS

CHAPTER REVIEW

Learning Objectives

After studying Chapter 3 you should be able to:

1. Describe the major features of the Bill of Rights and understand how and why it applies to the states as well as the national government.

2. Explain how the First Amendment rights of free speech, press, and assembly have evolved and comment on the controversies surrounding these rights.

3. Explain how the Supreme Court has interpreted the religion clauses of the Constitution, citing key cases as examples.

4. Describe how the Constitution protects the rights of the accused and how the Supreme Court has interpreted these rights through key court cases.

5. Discuss the controversy over the right to privacy, particularly as it relates to abortion.

6. Differentiate between the various concepts of equality and the constitutional interpretation of equality.

7. Trace the history of racial discrimination in America and the legal attempts to reduce discrimination.

8. Explain how the voting franchise has been extended in the United States, particularly in terms of the Voting Rights Act of 1965.

9. Describe the efforts to eliminate sex discrimination in the United States.

10. Compare and contrast how discrimination has affected American Indians, Latinos, immigrants, the elderly, the poor, and Americans with disabilities in the United States.

Chapter Outline and Summary

I. Introduction

    A. The framers of the Constitution wanted not only a strong and effective government, but also one that would guard the rights of a free people.

    B. A civil liberty is a legally protected freedom to act or not to act, and to be free from unwarranted governmental intrusion.

    C. Civil rights encompass participatory rights, which are citizens' legal rights to participate in society and politics on an equal footing with others.

II. The Bill of Rights: Securing the Blessings of Liberty

    A. Applying the Bill of Rights to the States

        1. Individual liberties are protected in the Bill of Rights.

        2. The Bill of Rights at first did not apply to the states.

        3. Through a process of incorporation, the Supreme Court used the Fourteenth Amendment as a vehicle for making the Bill of Rights applicable to the states.

    B. The Fragility of Civil Liberties

        1. Civil liberties have meant more in some years than in others.

        2. Americans do not agree on the rights the Constitution should protect.

        3. Maintenance of civil liberties rests on rules and institutions and the attitudes and values of the people.

III. Free Expression: Speech, Press, and Assembly

    A. Introduction

        1. Freedoms of speech, press, and assembly are found in the First Amendment.

        2. These liberties all involve forms of expression.

    B. The Value of Free Expression

        1. It is necessary to the political process.

        2. It allows the dominant wisdom of the day to be challenged.

        3. It aids self-development.

        4. Free expression may not produce the wisest policy and can threaten social and political stability.

C. The Test of Freedom

    1. Examples of free speech suppression included the Sedition Act of 1798 and instances during the Civil War, World War I, and the red scare that followed.

    2. The Supreme Court's clear and present danger test prohibited speech only when it would result in imminent harmful consequences (Holmes/Brandeis).

    3. The bad tendency test, used for a short time, would prohibit speech even if it did not result in an immediate harm.

D. Gags

    1. The Court is unlikely to approve a prior restraint, censorship before publication.

    2. The Court only rarely approves a pretrial gag even if it protects the right to a fair trial.

E. Obscenity and Libel

    1. The Court regards obscenity as unprotected speech because of the public view that it is deleterious.

    2. The Court has applied the "contemporary community standards" test (*Miller v. California*) to define obscenity.

    3. Libel, which involves character defamation, is not generally protected by the First Amendment.

    4. In *New York Times v. Sullivan* the Court stated that premeditated malice must be proved before libel exists.

    5. Some argue that the threat of libel makes journalists wary and keeps them from doing a thorough job, while others believe it keeps journalists honest and acts as a check on their power.

F. Freedom of Assembly and Symbolic Speech

    1. Symbolic speech, such as a sit-in, has been held as unconstitutional when the mode of expression (not the ideas) is considered harmful.

    2. The Court has upheld the right of individuals to deface the flag as a symbol of protest and barred Congress from criminalizing flag-burning.

IV. Religious Freedom

A. Religion and the Constitution

    1. The United States is very diverse religiously.

    2. The free exercise clause preserves religion free of government interference.

    3. The establishment clause keeps government from becoming the tool of one religious group against others.

B. Aid to Sectarian Schools

    1. The Court has allowed some public aid to sectarian schools if they pass certain requirements under the *Lemon* test.

C. Prayer in the Public Schools

    1. *Engel v. Vitale* outlawed mandatory prayer in public schools.

    2. Although creating controversy, the Court has been firm in its opposition to state sponsored religious activities.

D. Religious Observances in Official Settings

    1. Outside of schools, the Court has been more willing to allow religious practices in official settings.

    2. The Court has placed some limits on official observances of religious holidays, not permitting any implication of endorsement of a religion.

E. Free Exercise of Religion

    1. Problems occur when application of a law is counter to a religious tenet (as in the Amish and compulsory education).

    2. When actions based on religious belief run afoul of criminal law, the latter prevails (as in the American Indian Church's use of peyote).

V. Fundamentals of American Criminal Justice

A. Introduction

    1. The American criminal justice system requires that legal guilt be proven and that proper criminal procedure be followed.

    2. Conflict often occurs when attempting to balance the values of individual fairness and crime control.

B. Presumption of Innocence and Notice of Charges

    1. Presumption of innocence lays the burden of proving guilt on the government.

    2. The prosecution must also demonstrate *mens rea,* or criminal intent, allowing insanity as a defense.

    3. A suspect is entitled to know precisely what charges the state intends to level or prove so he or she can present a defense.

    4. Ex post facto laws and bills of attainder are forbidden by the Constitution.

C. Limits on Searches and Arrests

   1. In many searches and some arrests, the Fourth Amendment requires a judge-issued warrant based on probable cause.

   2. The exclusionary rule disallows evidence gained as a result of violating the suspect's rights.

D. Assistance of Counsel and Protection Against Self-incrimination

   1. The Fifth Amendment prohibits the use of interrogations to coerce confessions and protects suspects from having to testify at their own trials.

   2. *Miranda v. Arizona* excluded all confessions unless police informed the suspect of their Miranda rights.

   3. Many suspects decide to plea bargain, by which they confess to obtain a lighter sentence.

   4. Although the Sixth Amendment guarantees the right to counsel, until the 1970s defendants who could not afford a lawyer often went unrepresented.

   5. Today, the court appoints counsel when a defendant cannot afford one.

   6. Public defenders and less expensive lawyers have heavy case loads, resulting in a large number of plea bargains.

E. Limits on Punishment

   1. The Eighth Amendment prohibits "cruel and unusual punishment."

   2. Although the Court does not consider the death penalty unconstitutional, states vary widely in how they use it.

   3. Many argue that the death penalty is racially discriminatory and the process is flawed.

VI. A Right to Privacy

A. Introduction

   1. The Ninth Amendment provides the basis for civil liberties not specifically mentioned in the Constitution.

B. The Abortion Controversy

   1. *Roe v. Wade* recognized a woman's right to abortion in the first and second trimesters allowing states to ban abortions only in the third trimester.

   2. Since *Roe*, attempts to limit abortion failed until *Webster v. Reproductive Health Services* gave states greater power to restrict abortion without overturning *Roe*.

C. Personal Autonomy and Sexual Orientation

   1. Controversy continues regarding government's right to rule on people's choices about sexual relations.

VII. Racial Equality

   A. Equality: A Concept in Dispute

      1. Policies promoting equality of opportunity would remove barriers of discrimination that existed in the past.

      2. Policies promoting equality of condition would reduce or eliminate handicaps caused by lingering effects of past discriminations.

      3. Policies promoting equality of result, such as affirmative action programs, would guarantee equal outcomes.

         a. Suspect classifications that discriminate against racial or ethnic minorities.

         b. Laws that burden or penalize someone in exercising what the Court considers a "fundamental right."

   B. The Legacy: Slavery and Third-Class Citizenship

      1. The Civil War ended slavery (Thirteenth Amendment) and ushered in several civil rights acts during Reconstruction.

      2. *Plessy v. Ferguson* legitimized segregation through the separate-but-equal doctrine.

      3. Every aspect of life in the South became racially segregated by law.

      4. Southern politicians systematically excluded African Americans from the political process.

      5. African Americans were shortchanged in the delivery of public services, especially education.

   C. The Counterattack

      1. The NAACP and its Legal Defense Fund pressed for desegregation through the courts.

      2. *Brown v. Board of Education of Topeka* overturned *Plessy* and the separate-but-equal doctrine.

   D. Putting *Brown* to Work: The Law and Politics of Integration

      1. Several factors hampered *Brown's* implementation.

         a. Some federal judges in the South opposed integration.

         b. Local school boards opposed *Brown*.

       c. Many feared a hostile reaction from whites.

       d. The Court lacked initial support from Congress, the White House, and much of the legal community.

   2. The Civil Rights Act of 1964 and the Elementary and Secondary Education Act of 1965 furthered integration.

E. The Continuing Effects of *Brown*

   1. Until the 1970s the Court focused on eliminating *de jure* segregation (by law).

   2. After 1971 the Court focused on *de facto* segregation (unofficial) through controversial policies such as redrawing school attendance zones and busing.

   3. Social segregation, especially in terms of residence, remains a fact in many areas of the nation.

F. Affirmative Action

   1. No firm consensus exists on the merits of affirmative action.

   2. The use of quotas in applying affirmative action led to charges of reverse discrimination.

   3. *Regents of the University of California v. Bakke* outlawed racial quotas but permitted the use of race as one factor in admissions.

   4. The legal limits to affirmative action remains a subject of debate. (See "Contemporary Controversies: How Much Affirmative Action?")

G. Voting Rights

   1. The Voting Rights Act of 1965 is the most important voting legislation ever enacted by Congress.

   2. Advance clearance is required prior to any change in a locale's electoral system, protecting changes in African American voting power.

   3. An *existing* electoral arrangement that has a racially discriminatory effect also violates the law (1982 Amendment to 1965 Voting Rights Act).

   4. African American voter registration has increased dramatically since 1965.

VIII. Sexual Equality

A. The Legacy

   1. In the nineteenth century, the wife had no legal existence apart from her husband.

   2. The suffrage movement resulted in the Nineteenth Amendment giving women the right to vote in 1920.

B. Gender to the Forefront

   1. Sex discrimination became an issue in the 1960s and 1970s as more women increased their education and career opportunities.

   2. Several laws were passed outlawing sexual discrimination.

   3. Comparable worth in wage scales, would mandate equal pay for jobs of equal value and require congressional or state action.

IX. Other Americans and Civil Rights

   A. American Indians

      1. Although few in number, American Indians suffer high rates of sickness, poverty, illiteracy, and unemployment.

      2. American Indians have been granted more rights and greater control over their own affairs reflecting a heightened ethnic pride and political awareness.

   B. Latinos

      1. Latinos are the nation's fastest-growing and largest minority.

      2. Where necessary, ballots must be printed in Spanish and bilingual education must be provided.

      3. Latinos have become an important political force.

   C. Immigrants

      1. Legal immigration has been limited since 1921.

      2. Illegal aliens are a target for discrimination and violence.

      3. The Immigration Reform and Control Act gave legal residence to many illegal aliens and required employers to verify legal status but has resulted in discrimination against Latinos and Asians.

   D. Disabled Americans

      1. Disabled Americans are the nation's largest (over 43 million) minority group.

      2. The Americans with Disabilities Act (1990) bans discrimination in employment and places of public accommodation.

X. Liberties and Rights in the Constitutional Framework

   A. Introduction

      1. Civil rights and liberties are part of the framework of American constitutional government.

2. Much of what government and people have done in recent decades has been driven by an intolerance of inequality.

XI. Summary

Key Terms, Concepts, and Personalities

After studying Chapter 3 you should be able to identify and describe the significance of:

affirmative action

bad tendency test

bill of attainder

Brown v. Board of Education of Topeka

capital case

Civil Rights Act of 1964

clear and present danger test

comparable worth

cruel and unusual punishment

de facto segregation

de jure segregation

Eighth Amendment

equal protection clause

equality of condition

equality of opportunity

equality of result

establishment clause

exclusionary rule

ex post facto laws

felony

Fifth Amendment

First Amendment

Fourteenth Amendment

Fourth Amendment

free exercise clause

incitement test

legal guilt

Lemon test

libel

Miranda rights

misdemeanor

NAACP

Ninth Amendment

obscenity

plea bargain

presumption of innocence

prior restraint

probable cause

reverse discrimination

Roe v. Wade

separate-but-equal doctrine

Sixth Amendment

symbolic speech

Thirteenth Amendment

Voting Rights Act of 1965

warrant

TESTING YOUR UNDERSTANDING

Completion

1. The purpose of protecting _____ _____ is to place certain practices beyond government's reach.

2. The Fourteenth Amendment laid the groundwork to make the Bill of Rights applicable to the _____.

3. Of the possible restrictions on speech today, the Supreme Court is least likely to approve a _____ _____.

4. A sit-in is an example of _____ speech.

5. The _____ clause keeps government from becoming the tool of one religious group against others.

6. The _____ _____ denies government the use of evidence gained as a result of violation of the suspect's rights.

7. A deal with a prosecutor to obtain a lighter sentence in exchange for a guilty plea is called a _____ _____.

8. The landmark case that recognized abortion as part of the constitutionally protected right to privacy was _____ v. _____.

9. Affirmative action programs are often aimed at achieving equality of _____.

10. "Unofficial" segregation is often called _____ segregation.

11. _____ _____ in wage scales would mandate equal pay for jobs of equal value.

12. An unintended consequence of the Immigration Reform and Control Act has been discrimination against persons of _____ and _____ descent.

Compare and Contrast

1. clear and present danger test and bad tendency test

2. obscenity and libel

3. free exercise clause and establishment clause

4. ex post facto laws and bill of attainder

5. warrant and probable cause

6. *Miranda* rights and plea bargain

7. capital cases, misdemeanors, and felonies

8. *Roe v. Wade* and *Webster v. Reproductive Health Services*

9. equality of opportunity, equality of condition, and equality of result

10. Civil Rights Act of 1964 and Elementary and Secondary Education Act of 1965

11. *de jure* segregation and *de facto* segregation

12. affirmative action and *Regents of the University of California v. Bakke*

13. Voting Rights Act of 1965 and the 1982 Amendment

True-False

1. The language of the Fourteenth Amendment has been used by the courts to apply the Bill of Rights to the states.   T   F

2. For the most part the Supreme Court considers obscenity as unprotected speech.   T   F

3. The Court has ruled that libel is specifically protected by the First Amendment.   T   F

4. The establishment clause forbids the creation of an official state religion.   T   F

5. When action based on religious belief runs counter to criminal law, the latter prevails.   T   F

6. A police officer must always present a warrant before any search is made.   T   F

7. Indigent people have no constitutional right to have state-appointed counsel in civil cases.   T   F

8. The Supreme Court has required the states to formulate uniform policies toward capital punishment.   T   F

9. *Roe v. Wade* prohibited virtually all restrictions on a woman's right to have an abortion during her first trimester of pregnancy.   T   F

10. Civil rights refers exclusively to one's specific constitutional rights.   T   F

11. The separate-but-equal doctrine was struck down by the Supreme Court in *Plessy v. Ferguson.*   T   F

12. Shortly after the Supreme Court case of *Brown v. Board of Education of Topeka* schools in the South were desegregated.   T   F

13. Public opinion polls have shown overwhelming popular support for affirmative action programs.   T   F

14. The Voting Rights Act of 1965 requires that any change in a locale's electoral system must be first cleared by the U.S. attorney general or the U.S. District Court for the District of Columbia.   T   F

15. Very few American Indians still live in reservations.   T   F

Multiple Choice

1. The Fourteenth Amendment:
    a. is directed to state governments.
    b. is precise about what is meant by liberty.
    c. was passed after the case of *Gitlow v. New York*.
    d. required another amendment to incorporate the Bill of Rights.

2. Which of the following statements does not reflect an important objective of free expression?
   a. It is necessary to the political process set up by the Constitution.
   b. It contributes to social and political stability.
   c. It allows the dominant wisdom of the day to be challenged.
   d. It aids self-development.

3. Regarding the issue of obscenity, the Supreme Court has:
   a. required scientific evidence that obscene materials are harmful.
   b. clearly defined its meaning.
   c. set a national standard for judging obscene materials.
   d. regarded it as unprotected speech.

4. An example of symbolic speech is:
   a. a sit-in.
   b. libel.
   c. obscenity.
   d. defamation of character.

5. Using the *Lemon* test criteria, the Supreme Court has approved aid to sectarian schools in the form of:
   a. transportation for field trips.
   b. state tax credits for tuition.
   c. textbook loans to pupils.
   d. teacher salary supplements.

6. The Supreme Court has approved all of the following except:
   a. paying a state legislature's chaplain out of public funds.
   b. letting the Amish take their children out of school after the eighth grade.
   c. the formation of a religious club at a public high school.
   d. letting members of the American Indian Church ingest peyote as part of a religious ritual.

7. *Mens rea* refers to:
   a. criminal procedure.
   b. criminal intent.
   c. presumption of innocence.
   d. legal guilt.

8. The exclusionary rule:
   a. allows retroactive application of criminal laws in certain cases.
   b. bypasses the procedural safeguards of the legal process when meting out punishment.
   c. denies government the use of evidence gained as a result of violation of the suspect's rights.
   d. allows the police to search a suspect without a warrant.

9. *Miranda* rights do not include the right to:
   a. remain silent.
   b. refuse a search if not presented with a warrant.
   c. have a lawyer present during interrogation.
   d. have a lawyer free of charge if the suspect cannot afford one.

10. The right to counsel is guaranteed in all cases except:
    a. capital cases.   c. felonies.
    b. misdemeanors.   d. civil cases.

11. Which of the following statements about capital punishment is false?
    a. The Court had declined to view capital punishment as a violation of the Eighth Amendment.
    b. States vary widely in terms of the minimum age of a defendant who may be sentenced to death.
    c. All fifty states allow capital punishment under certain conditions.
    d. none of the above

12. The Ninth Amendment:
    a. suggests that people have certain rights that are not specifically stated in the Constitution.
    b. protects the right to privacy.
    c. extends the rights granted in the Constitution to the states.
    d. prohibits cruel and unusual punishment.

13. *Roe v. Wade*:
    a. voided a state law prohibiting the use of birth control devices.
    b. outlawed the practice of abortion.
    c. prohibited virtually all restrictions on abortions during the first trimester.
    d. required the states to have their own policies on abortion.

14. *Webster v. Reproductive Health Services*:
    a. voided a state law prohibiting the use of birth control devices.
    b. made it clear that states could place restrictions on abortions.
    c. overturned *Roe v. Wade*.
    d. outlawed the practice of abortion.

15. To get around the Fifteenth Amendment, Southern legislatures often turned to discriminatory devices such as:
    a. poll taxes.
    b. literacy tests.
    c. the white primary.
    d. all of the above

16. Early attempts to undermine racial segregation took the form of:
    a. lawsuits to challenge the constitutionality of discrimination.
    b. legislative action led by liberal members of Congress.
    c. pressure on local city councils and state governments.
    d. widespread demonstrations and boycotts.

17. Quick implementation of the *Brown* decision was hampered by:
    a. opposition by federal judges in the South.
    b. opposition by local school boards.
    c. fear of hostile reaction by the local white community.
    d. all of the above

18. According to the Supreme Court, segregation between school districts is unconstitutional when:
    a. each district is composed of over 85 percent of one race.
    b. it is accompanied by large economic inequalities between the districts.
    c. there is evidence that school boards have caused the segregation between districts.
    d. educational opportunities are substantially different between the districts.

19. The Voting Rights Act of 1965 has had the effect of:
    a. declaring certain judgeships illegal.
    b. dramatically increasing African American voter registration in the South.
    c. mass election of African Americans to state and local offices in the South.
    d. all of the above

20. Sexual bias in employment and promotion practices was outlawed by:
    a. the Equal Pay Act of 1963.
    b. Title VII of the 1964 Civil Rights Act.
    c. Title IX of the 1972 Educational Amendments.
    d. the Equal Rights Amendment.

21. Comparable worth:
    a. is required by the Equal Pay Act.
    b. would become national policy under the Equal Rights Amendment.
    c. would mandate equal pay for jobs of equal value.
    d. involves preferential treatment for minorities.

22. Which of the following statements about American Indians is false?
    a. They compose less than one percent of the population.
    b. They suffer high rates of poverty and unemployment.
    c. They live primarily in large urban areas.
    d. They did not become American citizens until 1924.

23. The nation's fastest growing minority group consists of:
    a. Latinos.
    b. American Indians.
    c. Asians.
    d. the poor.

24. The Immigration Reform and Control Act of 1986:
    a. extended legal resident status to illegal aliens who arrived before January 1, 1982.
    b. requires employers to verify the citizenship or legal status of all job applicants.
    c. resulted in discrimination against persons of Latino or Asian descent.
    d. all of the above

25. The Americans with Disabilities Act of 1990:
    a. does not include individuals with mental disorders.
    b. bans discrimination in programs receiving federal financial assistance.
    c. bans discrimination in employment and places of public accommodation.
    d. classifies individuals with drug addiction as disabled Americans.

Essay

1. Explain how and why civil liberties are "fragile." Give examples to illustrate your answer.

2. Why is the right to free expression so important in a democracy and how might free expression be detrimental? Use examples involving controversies over such issues as prior restraint, obscenity, libel, and symbolic speech to illustrate your answer.

3. How have the two religion clauses been interpreted in regard to the issue of religion and schools, both sectarian and public?

4. Comment on the argument that criminal suspects have too many protections under the Bill of Rights. In what ways does the Bill of Rights protect accused persons and does this place too many restrictions on the ability of the police to do their job?

5. Explain what is meant by the exclusionary rule. Why has the exclusionary rule been a controversial issue? Use examples to illustrate the controversy.

6. Explain the different definitions of the term "equality." What is the equal protection clause and how has the Supreme Court interpreted it?

7. Explain what is meant by "third-class" citizenship for African Americans and how it was established after the Civil War.

8. How has racial segregation and discrimination been reduced in the United States. Explain the significance of key Supreme Court cases and acts of Congress in the fight against discrimination. Has racial discrimination been eliminated? What issues remain?

9. Summarize the pros and cons of the comparable worth issue. Present an argument for or against comparable worth.

Research Topics and Practical Applications

1. Choose a Supreme Court case discussed in this chapter involving a particular civil liberty. Read the majority and minority decisions in the case and summarize the arguments presented. What were the conflicting social values involved in the case? Do you agree or disagree with the decision? How might you have decided differently?

2. Using the *Statistical Abstract of the United States* and other sources collect crime statistics on the number of felonies and capital cases over the past ten years. What do the statistics tell you about the case load in the courts? How have convictions changed over time? Are conviction rates different between African Americans and whites, men and women, or different locales? Comment on how certain groups of people seem to have more civil liberties than others.

3. Choose two prominent civil rights leaders, such as Martin Luther King, Jr., Malcolm X, Jesse Jackson, or Louis Farrakhan. Research their lives and activities with regard to the civil rights movement. Write a paper that compares and contrasts their philosophy, teachings, political activities, and constituents. Which leader do you believe has been most effective and why? What challenges face civil rights leaders today?

ANSWER KEY

Completion

1. civil liberties
2. states
3. prior restraint
4. symbolic
5. establishment
6. exclusionary rule
7. plea bargain
8. *Roe v. Wade*
9. results
10. *de facto*
11. Comparable worth
12. Latino, Asian

True-False

1. T
2. T
3. F
4. T
5. T
6. F
7. T
8. F
9. T
10. F
11. F
12. F
13. F
14. T
15. F

Multiple Choice

1. a
2. b
3. d
4. a
5. c
6. d
7. b
8. c
9. b
10. d
11. c
12. a
13. c
14. b
15. d
16. a
17. d
18. c
19. d
20. b
21. c
22. c
23. a
24. d
25. c

Chapter 4

POLITICAL IDEOLOGIES

CHAPTER REVIEW

Learning Objectives

After studying Chapter 4 you should be able to:

1. Explain how and why ideology plays an important role in American political life.

2. Summarize the historical development of liberalism and conservatism in the United States and compare and contrast the main ideas behind each ideology.

3. Discuss the intellectual components of the more extreme ideologies of democratic socialism, and libertarianism and comment on their role in American politics.

Chapter Outline and Summary

I. Introduction

    A. Political ideology is an integrated set of political ideas about what constitutes the most equitable and just political order.

II. American Political Ideologies

    A. Introduction

        1. Most Americans identify with mainstream ideologies (liberal or conservative) that do not challenge the existing political order.

        2. Radical ideologies (democratic socialism and libertarianism) challenge much of the existing social and political order.

        3. Socialism and libertarianism operate within the democratic framework.

III. Liberalism

    A. Introduction

        1. Liberalism assumes that individuals are rational and capable of overcoming obstacles without resorting to violence.

        2. John Locke's contract theory of the state declares that the state gains its legitimacy from the people and is required to protect life, liberty, and property.

    B. Classical Liberalism: Thomas Jefferson and Andrew Jackson

        1. Nineteenth century classical liberalism believed that the government that governed least governed best.

        2. Jefferson and Jackson believed that a strong central government would promote a "moneyed aristocracy dangerous to the liberties of the country."

    C. Populism and Progressivism: The Repudiation of Classical Liberalism

        1. Populism called for further democratization of government and strengthening government's role in the economy.

        2. Progressivism (especially Theodore Roosevelt and Woodrow Wilson) supported government programs to ease the problems of industrialization, such as worker's compensation and the regulation of corporations and banks.

    D. Contemporary Liberalism: The Welfare State and Beyond

        1. Roosevelt's New Deal changed the constituency of liberalism and believed that government should ensure the economic well-being of the nation and provide basic material guarantees.

        2. Liberals today believe that government must protect individuals from the inequities of modern society and that strong government enhances individual freedom.

        3. Liberals see government as correcting the injustices of capitalism, not supplanting it.

        4. A benevolent government offers services to both the disadvantaged (unemployment insurance) and the middle class (Social Security), as occurred during Johnson's Great Society.

        5. In the 1980s, many liberals favored an industrial policy involving government, labor, and public interests.

        6. Liberals extend broad tolerance to different lifestyles and favor limiting government interference in individual rights.

        7. In foreign policy, liberals oppose interventionism and military solutions (except in case for human rights issues), supporting foreign aid, arms control, and reduced military budgets.

8. Liberals tend to be members of the Democratic Party because of their support for a wide range of liberal welfare programs.

9. Americans for Democratic Action (ADA) is the most prominent liberal pressure group.

E. Neoliberalism: Adjusting Liberalism to the Twenty-First Century

1. In recent decades liberalism shifted its focus somewhat from economic issues to social and foreign policy issues.

2. This shift caused liberals to lose support from certain groups and aggravated their ability to capture the presidency.

3. In response, neoliberals call for a shift in the emphasis of liberalism from the redistribution of wealth to the promotion of wealth.

4. Neoliberals direct their attention not to the expansion of government services but to their effective delivery, favoring reform in the size and cost of bureaucracy, entitlement programs, and military spending.

5. Traditional liberals criticize neoliberal emphasis on government efficiency and call for a return to populist ideas.

IV. Conservatism

A. Introduction

1. Conservatism emphasizes the value of tradition and established practices as guides for the future.

2. Edmund Burke's (1729–1797) conservative principles included:

a. The experience of past generations was the most reliable guide to good government.

b. A natural inequality among men meant that a ruling class of ability and property must control government.

B. Early American Conservatism: John Adams

1. Adams believed in the sanctity of private property but did not associate property with an aristocracy.

2. Adams favored a balanced government (as in the Constitution) to promote public virtue and curb private greed.

3. Conservatives favored limiting suffrage to men with property.

C. Conservatism and the Industrial Age: Herbert Spencer and William Graham Sumner

1. As America industrialized, conservatives no longer supported government's role in the economy but embraced laissez-faire economics.

2. Spencer and Sumner established the theory of social Darwinism, which stated that people should compete for survival so that superior individuals would win and better humanity.

3. Conservatism became the ideology of the business class with emphasis on the individual and limited government.

D. Contemporary Conservatism: A Response to the Welfare State

1. From 1933–1981, conservatism was measured more by what it was against than what it was for.

2. By the 1980s conservatism established its own agenda but still defended economic individualism against the growth of the welfare state.

3. Contemporary conservatives accept civil rights, but oppose quotas and affirmative action.

4. Contemporary conservatives believe the state must promote virtue and social responsibility and improve the moral climate of society.

5. Conservatism has been embraced by the more populist ideals of the working and middle classes.

6. Most conservatives belong to the Republican Party.

E. Neoconservatism in the Twenty-First Century

1. Neoconservatives consist of disenchanted liberals who believe the welfare state has become an intrusive paternalistic state.

2. Neoconservatives oppose quotas and busing, which cause class polarization, and higher taxes on the upper middle class, which emphasize economic redistribution over growth.

3. Neoconservatives support a modest welfare state with lower taxes on large incomes and less regulation to promote growth.

4. Neoconservatives have pushed for an empowerment agenda to assist the poor that emphasizes anti-bureaucratic market-oriented programs.

V. Ideological Challenges to the Status Quo

A. Democratic Socialism: A Radical Challenge to American Capitalism

1. Democratic socialism is an economic system in which the basic industries, banks, agricultural systems, and communication networks are owned by the government.

2. Democratic socialists advocate the adoption of socialism through peaceful, democratic means.

3. Central ideas include economic equality, government ownership of key infrastructure, limits on wealth and property, a universal welfare system, and government regulation of the economy.

4. The pre–New Deal Socialist Party was led by Eugene Debs, later succeeded by the Democratic Socialists of America, led by Michael Harrington.

5. Post–New Deal socialists favor guaranteed full employment, a public works program to rebuild America's infrastructure, and worker or community-owned businesses and factories.

6. Socialism has received very little public support in the United States and works to influence rather than control politics.

B. Libertarianism: A Revival of Classical Liberalism

1. Libertarianism believes that the state must be kept small with the essential role of government limited to the protection of human rights.

2. Libertarians oppose the interference of government in private lives, whether to regulate moral or economic life.

3. Libertarians favor nonintervention in the affairs of other nations.

4. The Libertarian Party and its ideas has influenced both the Republican and Democratic parties.

VI. Summary

Key Terms, Concepts, and Personalities

After studying Chapter 4 you should be able to identify and describe the significance of:

Americans for Democratic Action	libertarianism
classical liberalism	neoconservatism
conservatism	neoliberalism
contract theory	democratic socialism
political ideology	industrial policy
populism	laissez-faire economics
progressivism	liberalism
social Darwinism	

TESTING YOUR UNDERSTANDING

Completion

1. Classical liberals believed that the government that governed _____ governed _____.

2. Progressives supported government programs to ease the problems of _____.

3. _____ direct their attention not to the expansion of government services but to their effective delivery.

4. As America industrialized, conservatives embraced _____ economics, an economic system free of government control.

5. Contemporary conservatism remains at its core a defense of economic individualism against the growth of the _____ _____.

6. _____ argue that a properly constructed welfare state strengthens citizen's loyalty to the capitalist system.

7. The _____ _____ combined the elements of traditional conservatism and the populist belief that government was run by narrow, selfish interests.

8. Democratic socialists believe that a genuinely democratic society must produce equality of _____.

9. Libertarianism holds that the essential role of government should be only the protection of _____ _____.

10. _____ was an agrarian reform movement in the late nineteenth century that called for reforms such as a secret ballot and direct election of U.S. senators.

Compare and Contrast

1. liberalism and the contract theory of the state

2. John Locke, Thomas Jefferson, and Andrew Jackson

3. populism and progressivism

4. New Deal and Great Society

5. neoliberalism and neoconservatism

6. Edmund Burke and John Adams

7. laissez-faire economics and social Darwinism

8. Herbert Spencer and William Graham Sumner

9. neoconservatives and paleoconservatives

10. libertarianism and classical liberalism

True-False

1. Both liberals and conservatives accept most of the economic reforms of the New Deal. T F

2. Populists and progressives advocated economic reforms that would strengthen the government's role. T F

3. Contemporary liberals believe that a strong central government is necessary to reduce economic inequalities and enhance personal morality. T F

4. Neoliberals have repudiated the New Deal and Great Society legacies while emphasizing the promotion of wealth. T F

5. Edmund Burke believed that inequality among men meant that a ruling class of ability and property must control government. T F

6. Early American conservatives believed that only men who owned property should be allowed to vote. T F

7. Contemporary conservatism remains essentially an ideology of the wealthy upper class. T F

8. Like most conservative groups, the New Right defends and supports the major traditional institutions of contemporary America. T F

9. Democratic socialism essentially supports the democratic process and the ideals of capitalism. T F

10. Libertarians would support the repeal of laws forbidding prostitution, pornography, and gambling. T F

Multiple Choice

1. Political ideology is concerned with the:
   a. proper functions of government.
   b. issues of liberty and equality.
   c. distribution of goods and services.
   d. all of the above

2. Radical ideologies such as democratic socialism and libertarianism:
   a. accept the basic principles of capitalism as a successful economic system.
   b. challenge much of the existing social and political order.
   c. function outside of the democratic process.
   d. have become a major challenge to liberalism and conservatism in America.

3. According to John Locke's contract theory of the state:
   a. all men and women are allowed a voice in government.
   b. the state gains its legitimacy from the consent of the governed.
   c. a ruling class of ability and property must control government.
   d. the experience of past generations is the most reliable guide to good government.

4. Classical liberals such as Thomas Jefferson and Andrew Jackson believed:
   a. in a strong central government.
   b. that unregulated capitalism resulted in rule by a moneyed aristocracy.
   c. that liberty was the absence of government interference with the rights of citizens.
   d. that government expenditures should be limited to infrastructure projects such as roads and canals.

5. Populism and progressivism opposed the classical liberal belief that:
   a. a ruling class of ability and property should run government.
   b. the railroads, telegraph, and basic industries should be nationalized.
   c. the role of government should be limited.
   d. government should be further democratized by extending the franchise.

6. New Deal contemporary liberalism:
   a. changed the constituency of liberalism to include the entrepreneurial class.
   b. is based on the belief that government should provide basic material guarantees for every individual.
   c. favored a decreased role of government in the economy.
   d. repudiated the ideals of capitalism.

7. In the areas of national security and personal morality, liberals:
   a. seek to increase the role of government.
   b. show little tolerance to different lifestyles.
   c. support expanding the role of the CIA in foreign affairs.
   d. advocate arms control agreements.

8. Neoliberals:
   a. favor policies that call for greater government and business cooperation.
   b. support expanding the size and role of government unions.
   c. prefer reducing defense spending to military reforms.
   d. favor tying civil service and military benefits to the cost of living.

9. Edmund Burke believed that:
   a. each generation should remake society to fit the changing environment.
   b. society grew slowly and with purpose.
   c. there was a natural equality among men.
   d. government should listen to the public's appreciation of tradition and custom.

10. John Adams:
    a. agreed with Burke's association of property rights with a landed aristocracy.
    b. supported Jefferson's notion of the natural goodness of humankind.
    c. believed that laws and government are needed to promote public virtue and curb private greed.
    d. called for universal manhood suffrage.

11. According to William Graham Sumner, the two chief things that government has to deal with are:
    a. the property of men and the honor of women.
    b. military defense and civil liberties.
    c. social welfare and economic growth.
    d. crime and poverty.

12. Which of the following statements about contemporary conservatives is false?
    a. They defend economic individualism against the growth of the welfare state.
    b. They believe that the state must promote virtue and social responsibility.
    c. They challenge the idea of quotas and other affirmative action policies.
    d. They oppose the use of the popular referendum and other means of direct democracy.

13. Neoconservatives:
    a. support racial and sexual quotas.
    b. stress policies that lower taxes on large incomes.
    c. call for more regulation of business to promote economic growth.
    d. support the idea of the welfare state in principle, but not in practice.

14. The idea that religious traditions embodied in the church and family should be the basis of a stable and ordered society is held by:
    a. neoconservatives.
    b. neoliberals.
    c. paleoconservatives.
    d. contemporary conservatives.

15. The New Right:
    a. is composed largely of pro-business elites.
    b. defends the established institutions of America.
    c. believes the media is responsible for a decline in social morality.
    d. gained support in the late 1980s and early 1990s.

16. Democratic socialists believe in:
    a. a limit on individual wealth and property.
    b. equality of results.
    c. extensive governmental regulation of the economy.
    d. all of the above

17. Contemporary American socialists favor:
    a. increasing the work week to 45 hours so as to encourage economic growth.
    b. public ownership characterized by government owned and controlled businesses and factories.
    c. dismantling the New Deal welfare state.
    d. none of the above

18. The intellectual roots of libertarianism can be traced to:
    a. populism and progressivism.
    b. the philosophy of Edmund Burke.
    c. classical liberalism.
    d. the New Deal.

Essay

1. Explain what is meant by the term "political ideology." Which of the specific ideologies covered in this chapter is most appealing to you and why?

2. Compare and contrast classical liberalism to populism and progressivism. What historical events led to this change in the liberal philosophy?

3. How does contemporary liberalism differ from neoliberalism? Give examples of how the two differ in terms of general political philosophy and specific public policy alternatives.

4. How has American political conservatism changed throughout the years and how has it remained the same? Give examples of public policy choices to illustrate your answer.

5. Explain the basic ideas and policy choices of democratic socialism. Why has democratic socialism not taken hold in the United States like it has in parts of Europe?

Research Topics and Practical Applications

1. Write an essay describing your own personal political ideology. You may wish to start by jotting down your views and opinions on the major issues of the day such as abortion, military spending, busing, foreign aid, women's rights, affirmative action, social welfare, economic policy, etc. What patterns or common themes are apparent in your opinions of these issues? Where might your political ideology fit within the different ideologies covered in the chapter?

2. Several ideologies other than liberalism and conservatism exist on the fringe of American politics. The chapter examines socialism and libertarianism. Others might include fascism, Marxism or communism, racism, environmentalism, etc. Write a fact sheet about some of these alternative ideologies. Include the following:
   a. a basic definition of the ideology.
   b. a brief statement on the ideology's philosophy on the role of government in foreign and defense policy, economics, social welfare, and personal morality.
   c. a brief statement on the ideology's stand on some of the major political issues of the day.
   d. a list of the political parties, organizations, journals, and leaders that represent the ideology.
   e. a statement describing the tactics used by advocates of the political ideology to gain influence.
   f. a statement commenting on the extent of the ideology's popularity and influence in the United States.

ANSWER KEY

Completion

1. least, best
2. industrialization
3. Neoliberals
4. laissez-faire
5. welfare state
6. Neoconservatives
7. New Right
8. results
9. individual liberties
10. Populism

True-False

1. T
2. T
3. F
4. F
5. T
6. T
7. F
8. F
9. F
10. T

Multiple Choice

1. d
2. b
3. b
4. c
5. c
6. b
7. d
8. a
9. b
10. c
11. a
12. d
13. b
14. c
15. c
16. d
17. b
18. c

Chapter 5

PUBLIC OPINION AND POLITICAL PARTICIPATION

CHAPTER REVIEW

Learning Objectives

After studying Chapter 5 you should be able to:

1. Discuss the nature of public opinion in the United States in terms of the similarities and differences between the public's attitudes toward the political process.

2. Define political socialization and summarize the process and agents of political socialization in the United States.

3. Explain the variations in political socialization within the United States and cross-nationally.

4. Itemize the different forms of political participation in the United States and explain their significance.

5. Explain the impact and rationality of political participation.

Chapter Outline and Summary

I. Introduction

    A. What Americans think about politics is important because it determines, in part, how they act politically.

II. Public Opinion: What Americans Think About Politics

    A. The Character of Public Opinion

        1. Public opinion is a combination of the views, attitudes, and ideas held by individuals in the community.

        2. The public's opinions may be constant or dynamic.

3. Public opinions may represent intense or casual preferences.

4. For many Americans, politics seldom occupies their attention.

B. How Much Americans Care and Know About Politics

1. Surveys show that Americans have some interest in politics, but fall short of the democratic ideal.

2. Substantial percentages of the public are uninformed about some of the major political issues of the time.

C. What Americans Hold in Common

1. Most Americans are proud of their country and emotionally attached to its symbols.

2. Americans have a positive image of their country's political, social, and economic institutions.

3. Americans tend to believe in the equality of all people.

4. The single thing that makes Americans proudest of their country is its commitment to freedom.

5. Most Americans have a strong commitment to government rule by the consent of the majority.

6. Americans are committed to capitalism and free enterprise as idealized in the values of hard work, private property, economic competition, and profit.

D. Where Americans Differ

1. The Meaning of Equality
   a. Americans tend to lean away from equality of result.
   b. Some Americans do not accept racial or sexual equality.

2. Limits of Freedom
   a. Americans are divided on their commitment to the freedom of expression on some subjects such as anti-religious or communist ideas.

3. Majority Rule versus Minority Rights
   a. Americans disagree on the limits that should be placed on the right to vote.

4. Free Enterprise in Practice
   a. Americans are divided over their concern about business practices and the degree to which businesses should be regulated.

5. Political Ideology
   a. Many Americans do not think about politics in ideologically coherent terms.
   b. Although essentially centrist, there is growing evidence that American public opinion is shifting to the right.

      c. Americans are either not familiar with the basic notion of liberalism versus conservatism or have disparate conceptions of what they mean.

      d. Americans tend to respond to political issues on an individual basis or act as an echo chamber, responding to politicians at the level on which they are addressed.

    6. Political Socialization

      a. Political Socialization is the process by which citizens acquire politically relevant knowledge, beliefs, attitudes, and patterns of behavior.

      b. Political socialization is a long and complicated process and is important to both stability and change in American politics.

E. The Processes of Political Socialization

    1. Social learning theory

      a. Learning through psychological attachments or identifications.

    2. Transfer theory

      a. Carrying over attitudes developed in a narrower setting.

    3. Cognitive development theory

      a. Learning is dependent on the stage of an individual's mental development.

F. The Agents of Political Socialization

    1. The Family

      a. The family has the first chance at political influence. Although politics is not a top priority in most families, most children adopt the same party preference as their parents.

      b. Family influence on political attitudes is greatest when attitudes relate to topics regularly discussed but political differences between parents and children are common.

    2. The School

      a. School is an important agent for information about politics.

      b. Schools promote feelings about social and political involvement through relationships and activities.

      c. The effect of school is gradual and subtle.

    3. Peer Groups

      a. Peer groups are groups of people, roughly equal in social position, who interact with one another.

      b. Social pressures on group members to conform can be strong.

      c. Peer group pressure can have mixed results.

4. Religion
    a. Religion can impact on political values.
    b. Protestants tend to be more conservative, Catholics more liberal, and Jews the most liberal.
G. The Development of Political Self
    1. A child's first political thought is a psychological attachment with America and a sense of authority personified in the president and police.
    2. As the result of exposure to school, children's conceptions of politics become less personal, more institutional, more realistic, and less partisan.
    3. In adolescence and early adulthood individuals establish a political identity and are strongly affected by major political and social events.
    4. During adulthood, political socialization evolves with the changing needs, concerns, and environments of the individual.

H. Diversity in Socialization
    1. Subsocieties, particularly African Americans, Latinos, and Asians, have exhibited distinctive political subcultures in America.
    2. Although the differences are fading, regions (particularly the South) have constituted distinctive political subcultures.
    3. Although historically women were socialized to be less politically oriented than men, this is changing in recent years with more women expressing an interest in politics and running for office.

III. Political Participation

A. Motives for Political Participation
    1. People with a strong sense of political efficacy and duty are more involved in politics.
    2. People with a strong party identification are more likely to participate in politics.
    3. Social motivations often lead to political participation.

B. Forms of Participation
    1. Much political activity is related to campaigns and elections (see Chapter 7) and interest groups and political parties (see Chapter 6).
    2. Paying attention to politics is a simple form of participation.
    3. Contacting public officials through letters, personally, or petitions is one of the most direct, but less frequent forms of political participation.

4. Protest is a form of political participation within or beyond the law, including marches and rallies, boycotts, picketing, political violence, and politically motivated crimes.

5. As in the case of civil disobedience and passive resistance, the line between legitimate and illegitimate political protest is sometimes hard to define.

C. Differences in Participation

1. Verba and Nie identified six categories of citizen participation: inactives, voting specialists, parochial participants, communalists, campaigners, and complete activists.

2. Since different kinds of people participate differently, public officials get different impressions of public opinion depending on which forms of participation they pay attention to.

D. The Impact of Political Participation

1. The relationship between opinion and policy is relatively loose because many people do not know what they want, there are many publics, and there are many constraints on policy.

2. The relationship is likely to be strong only when there is a clearly expressed body of opinion on a salient issue.

IV. Summary

Key Terms, Concepts, and Personalities

After studying Chapter 5 you should be able to identify and describe the significance of:

agents of socialization
civil disobedience
party identification
passive resistance

political efficacy
political socialization
public opinion
sense of duty

TESTING YOUR UNDERSTANDING

Completion

1. Although Americans profess a belief in equality, they seem to lean away from equality of
   _____.

2. What people can learn about politics depends on the stage of their mental development is
   an example of what psychologists call _____ _____
   _____.

3. Groups of people, roughly equal in social position, who interact with one another are called
   _____ _____.

4. As children grow, their idealization of political authority fades to _____.

5. _____ _____ is a person's sense of being able to
   accomplish something politically.

6. An act of _____ _____ is a deliberate violation of the
   law as a means of asserting the illegitimacy of the law or calling attention to a higher moral
   principle.

7. According to the text, voter turnout in the U.S. generally has been _____.

Compare and Contrast

1. constant and dynamic facets of public opinion

2. liberals and conservatives

3. social learning, transfer, and cognitive development theories

4. process and agents of political socialization

5. internal efficacy and external efficacy

6. civil disobedience and passive resistance

7. inactives, voting specialists, parochial participants, communalists, campaigners, and
   complete activists

True-False

1. The public's high degree of interest in politics is substantiated by their high level of knowledge of politics. T F

2. Americans tend to support equality of opportunity over equality of result. T F

3. The effect of school as an agent of political socialization is sudden and dynamic as the child enters grade school. T F

4. Once in school, children tend to become less partisan. T F

5. Political socialization differs widely between distinctive political subcultures in the United States. T F

6. The highest rates of political activity are among people with a strong commitment to a political party. T F

7. One of the most common methods of political participation in the United States is the direct contact of public officials. T F

8. Most studies have shown a strong relationship between public opinion and public policy. T F

9. Newspapers had very little influence in the United States during the eighteenth and nineteenth centuries. T F

Multiple Choice

1. Public opinion surveys that rate how well the president is handling the job:
    a. are not affected by political events.
    b. tend to remain consistent throughout a president's term.
    c. can vary significantly over time.
    d. are unreliable due to the public's lack of knowledge about politics.

2. A 1998 survey found out that a plurality of the public says they follow government and public affairs:
    a. most of the time.
    b. some of the time.
    c. only now and then.
    d. hardly at all.

3. Most Americans:
   a. have somewhat negative images of their form of government.
   b. do not have a strong emotional attachment to the symbols of their country, such as the flag.
   c. have positive images about their country's political, social, and economic institutions.
   d. have less confidence in their government than their European counterparts.

4. In recent years, American public opinion has:
   a. shifted to the right.
   b. shifted to the left.
   c. stayed essentially centrist.
   d. has become less ideologically oriented.

5. The theory suggesting that there are some things that can be learned only early in life and other things that can be learned only later in life is called:
   a. response reinforcement theory.
   b. social learning theory.
   c. transfer theory.
   d. cognitive development theory.

6. Research indicates that the transmission of political attitudes from parents to their offspring is substantial only when:
   a. attitudes relate to topics that regularly come up in family discussions.
   b. there is a strong sense of party identification among the parents.
   c. the children reach their teenage years.
   d. the children are very young.

7. While an important teacher of information about politics is the school, the most important source of political values is:
   a. the mass media.
   b. peer groups.
   c. the family.
   d. all of the above

8. The first political thoughts acquired by a small child is a:
   a. psychological attachment to America.
   b. primitive sense of party identification.
   c. sense of external authority above parental authority.
   d. all of the above

9. Major political and social events seem to have the most powerful and lasting effect on those who experience them in their:
    a. grade school years.
    b. teens and early twenties.
    c. thirties and forties.
    d. fifties and sixties.

10. The largest substantially different subculture in the United States is:
    a. African Americans.
    b. Latinos.
    c. the South.
    d. women.

11. All of the following are factors that motivate people to participate in politics except a:
    a. low sense of political efficacy.
    b. high sense of civic duty.
    c. strong sense of political identification.
    d. desire for social rewards.

12. Acts of civil disobedience have been justified on the basis of:
    a. legality.
    b. effectiveness.
    c. morality.
    d. popularity.

13. The percent of Americans who say that they have themselves broken the law in a protest for a political or social cause is _____.
    a. 1%
    b. 2%
    c. 5%
    d. 10%

14. According to Verba and Nie, the category of citizen participation that comprises about 4% of the population, consists of mainly lower-status groups, Catholics, and urban dwellers, and shows little partisan or ideological involvement, is:
    a. inactives.
    b. parochial participants.
    c. communalists.
    d. campaigners.

15. According to Verba and Nie, the most common form of participation in all democracies is:
    a. contacting officials.
    b. protests.
    c. campaigning.
    d. voting.

16. According to the rational actor model, which of the following activities would be considered the most rational and effective form of political participation?
    a. voting
    b. letter writing to public officials
    c. collective activities
    d. political assassination

Essay

1. Explain how Americans are at the same time similar and different in their attitudes toward fundamental political matters such as equality, freedom, consent of the governed, and the free enterprise system.

2. What is the nature of political ideology in the United States, how has it changed over time, and what do liberal and conservative mean to the American public?

3. Who are the primary agents of political socialization and how do they affect the development of the political self?

4. What are the different forms of political protests "within and beyond the law," who are most likely to participate in them, how might they be justified, and could they ever be considered a rational strategy?

Research Topics and Practical Application

1. Write an autobiographical account of your personal political socialization process. How did the various agents of socialization mold your present political attitudes? In particular, how did your family (especially your parents), school (particularly courses in civics or American government), peer groups, and television influence your political thinking? What was the first political event you can remember in your life time? Has any particular individual or event had a significant influence on your political beliefs or behavior?

ANSWER KEY

Completion

1. results
2. cognitive development theory
3. peer groups
4. realism
5. Political efficacy
6. civil disobedience
7. declining

True-False

1. F
2. T
3. F
4. T
5. T
6. T
7. F
8. F
9. F

Multiple Choice

1. c
2. a
3. c
4. a
5. d
6. a
7. c
8. d
9. b
10. a
11. a
12. c
13. b
14. b
15. d
16. c

Chapter 6

POLITICS AND THE MEDIA

CHAPTER REVIEW

Learning Objectives

After studying Chapter 6 you should be able to:

1. Explain mass media/journalists and the different formats media comes in.

2. Discuss the constitutional basis for the press as it relates to the First Amendment.

3. Understand the Federal Communications Commission (FCC) and the role it plays when dealing with the electronic media.

4. Discuss and explain FCC regulations.

5. Discuss how the media is a vehicle of direct communication to America.

6. Explain how the media can make issues and serve as a talent scout.

7. Understand the relationship that the media has with politicians and how the media receives information from government officials.

8. Discuss the bias of the media as it relates to deciding what becomes news and how it becomes news.

Chapter Outline and Summary

I. Introduction

   A. Mass Media—newspapers, magazines, radio, television, and the Internet.

   B. Journalists—people who gather, write, and report the news for mass media.

II. The "Fifth Branch"

A. The Dynamics of an Industry

    1. Newspapers

       a. Part of the American culture from the beginning.

       b. They rapidly grew because of telegraphy, better presses, lower costs and increased literacy.

    2. Magazines

       a. Became popular in the nineteenth century.

    3. Radio

       a. Began in 1920.

       b. Within 10 years, radios became common household appliances.

    4. Cable Services

       a. Began in the 1970s.

       b. Today, over 95 million televisions are equipped with some kind of cable service.

       c. Several new cable networks are exclusively for news.

       d. By 2001, cable network news had surpassed the broadcast networks.

    5. Americans and the Media

       a. Average American spends over 60 minutes each day with some kind of news media.

       b. Eighty percent of all Americans report that they receive some news on a daily basis.

       c. Older Americans are the most likely to be aware of televised news, while younger Americans prefer the Internet.

B. The Constitutional Basis of the Press

    1. The First Amendment guarantees freedom of the press.

    2. The Constitution creates the opportunity for the press to play an active role in public affairs.

    3. What type of role is up to the reporters, editors and publishers.

C. The Federal Communications Commission

    1. Some news media branches are more protected by the Constitution than others.

    2. Electronic journalism operates under legal restraints that do not apply to print journalism.

3. Radio and television forced a choice for Congress:

    a. No regulation.

    b. Government owned entities.

    c. Congress chose the middle road of private ownership under government supervision.

4. Initial regulation was given to the Department of Commerce.

5. Congress then created the Federal Radio Commission in 1927.

6. Present regulation of all wired and wireless communication is the responsibility of the Federal Communications Commission.

    a. FCC has five commissioners appointed by the president for seven-year terms.

    b. The FCC has currently adopted the view that the marketplace should dictate development of the industry and the Commission should stay focused on licensing, frequencies, and regulation.

D. The Equal Time Rule

1. The Equal Time Rule requires radio and television stations to give or sell equivalent time to one political candidate if the station has given or sold time to another candidate for that office.

E. The Fairness Doctrine

1. The Fairness Doctrine used to require radio and television stations to devote some airtime to a balanced discussion of public issues.

2. The FCC abolished this regulation in 1987, citing constitutional issues as well as the fact that the expansion of cable had undercut the rationale for the rule.

F. Regulating the Internet

1. The FCC is responsible for regulating interstate and international communication within the U.S., but currently its jurisdiction does not extend to global communications such as the Internet.

III. Politics and the Press

A. Direct Communication: The Media as Vehicles

1. Recent presidents have used the media to directly communicate with the American people.

B. Political Knowledge and Attitudes: The Media as Gatekeepers

   1. As gatekeepers, the media determines what the American people will know about.

   2. The mass media influences political attitudes by contributing to emotions and impressions.

C. Issues Making and Issue Reporting: The Media as Spotlights

   1. Spotlights—when journalists talk about their work as if television, newspapers, and the Internet were mirrors of society.

   2. Priming—occurs when the news media, especially television, set the terms by which the public judges its leaders.

D. Candidates and Campaigns: The Media as Talent Scouts

   1. Political candidates are treated as Hollywood stars and their political runs as horse races.

   2. Favorable stories equal free advertising for candidates.

E. Believability

   1. Believability—whether people are inclined to accept what they read and see as true.

   2. Believability of news reporting makes it more important politically.

IV. Tools of the Trade: Politicians and the "Fifth Branch"

A. Introduction

   1. The relationship between politicians and the media is symbiotic: each one contributes to the needs of the other.

B. Access

   1. Journalists rely on candidates and officials for access to news and sources.

   2. Leaks—the deliberate release of information by an official to a journalist for a specific purpose.

   3. Exclusive—an interview that an official or other individual grants to one or more journalists that provides information not generally made available to all media.

C. Public Announcements

   1. News release—a story written by a press agent for distribution to the media.

   2. Press conference—when candidates answer questions given by the journalists.

   3. News briefing—an announcement or explanation of policy to the media.

D.   Other Media Events

    1.   Visual—an image or series of images representing news in action.

        a.   Visual depictions carry more impact than words alone.

        b.   Example: a visual shot of a politician campaigning for votes.

    2.   Photo opportunities—events scheduled to give newspaper reporters and television crews a chance to photograph someone.

E.   A Right to Know?

    1.   How much access should the media have to military operations?

V.   Are the Media Biased?

A.   The Journalists

    1.   News is influenced by the people who write it.

    2.   Journalists have attitudes and outlooks that affect what they write.

    3.   Journalists are suspicious of politicians and the people in political power.

    4.   Journalists must have depth and evenhandedness in their news coverage.

B.   Deciding What Becomes News

    1.   Agenda setting—the process by which the news media select and focus on a small number of stories from a larger number of possibilities.

    2.   Some events, such as natural disasters and political turning points, are destined to become news.

    3.   Attention-getting stories and economics also plays a role in what stories the media covers.

    4.   Journalistic ethics play a role as well.

C.   Deciding How the News Appears

    1.   Framing—the way in the media presents a story, consisting of angle, tone, and point of view.

    2.   Media executives look at circulation figures and Nielsen ratings to determine what stories will be reported on.

D.   The Impact of the Visual

    1.   The visual has become a factor in the selection of stories and in the way those stories will be presented. Stories that can be easily visualized are given preference.

2. Visuals allow the public to actually see political candidates and their characteristics.

   E. A Public Trust

   1. The media has an obligation to report news accurately.

VI. Summary

Key Terms, Concepts, and Personalities

After studying Chapter 6 you should be able to identify and describe the significance of:

agenda setting	mass media
backgrounders	news briefing
equal-time rule	news release
exclusive	photo opportunity
fairness doctrine	press conference
Federal Communications Commission (FCC)	priming
fifth branch	shield laws
framing	sound bites
journalists	visual
leak	

TESTING YOUR UNDERSTANDING

Completion

1. People who gather, write, and report the news for the mass media are called

   _____.

2. The equal-time rule requires _____ and _____ stations to give or sell equivalent time to one political candidate if the station has given or sold time to another candidate for that office.

3. The Federal Communications Commission is an agency of the national government that regulates the _____ industry in the United States.

4. The _____ _____ was a regulation of the FCC that required radio and television stations to devote some airtime to a balanced discussion of public issues.

5. The fairness doctrine was abolished in _____.

6. Priming occurs when the news media, especially _____, set the terms by which the public judges its leaders.

7. The deliberate release of information by an official to a journalist for a specific purpose is called a _____.

8. A news release is a story written by a press agent for distribution to the _____.

9. The press is sometimes called the _____ _____ of government.

10. _____ _____ protect the identity of journalists' news sources or their knowledge of criminal acts.

Compare and Contrast

1. different kinds of mass media (newspapers, television, etc.)

2. FCC regulations

3. media as a vehicle of direct communication and as a talent scout

4. spotlights and priming

5. leaks, exclusives, news releases, press conferences, and news briefings

6. framing and visuals

True-False

1. Visuals allow the public to see political candidates and their characteristics. T F

2. Picturing is the way in the media presents a story, consisting of angle, tone, and point of view. T F

3. Journalistic ethics does not play a role in the bias of the media. T F

4. The process by which the news media select and focus on a small number of stories from a larger number of possibilities is known as agenda setting. T F

5. Economics plays a role in what stories the media will cover. T F

6. The bias of the media is affected by the attitudes and outlooks of journalists. T F

7. A visual is a scheduled event to give newspaper reporters and television crews a chance to photograph someone. T F

8. Many world leaders, including the president of the United States, often depend on Cable Network News as a more accurate source of information than their own official sources. T F

9. Increased access to the mass media has resulted in greater knowledge about news events and public affairs. T F

10. Radio and television operate under legal restraints that do not apply to print journalism. T F

Multiple Choice

1. An image or series of images representing news in action are called:
   a. frames.
   b. visuals.
   c. pictures.
   d. stop shots.

2. An announcement or explanation of policy to the media is called a:
   a. news briefing.
   b. press conference.
   c. news release.
   d. news framing.

3. A story written by a press agent for distribution to the media is called a:
   a. news briefing.
   b. press conference.
   c. news release.
   d. news framing.

4. When candidates answer questions given by journalists, they are at a:
   a. news briefing.
   b. press conference.
   c. news release.
   d. news framing.

5. A leak is what type of a release of information by an official to a journalist for a specific purpose?
    a. accidental
    b. involuntary
    c. deliberate
    d. mistaken

6. Whether people are inclined to accept what they read and see as true is called:
    a. selective attention.
    b. acceptability.
    c. perceived tune-out.
    d. believability.

7. The media determines what the American people will know about by being:
    a. key masters.
    b. gatekeepers.
    c. goaltenders.
    d. watch guards.

8. Favorable stories equal free advertising for:
    a. candidates.
    b. journalists.
    c. television.
    d. radio.

9. The mass media influences political attitudes by contributing to:
    a. truths.
    b. rumors.
    c. emotions.
    d. ratings.

10. Recently, this group of people have used the media to directly communicate with the American people.
    a. presidents
    b. mayors
    c. journalists
    d. executives

11. This FCC rule required radio and television stations to devote some airtime to a balanced discussion of public issues.
    a. equal-time rule
    b. equal-time doctrine
    c. airtime doctrine
    d. fairness doctrine

12. This FCC rule requires radio and television stations to give or sell equivalent time to one political candidate if the station has given or sold time to another candidate for that office.
    a. equal-time rule
    b. equal-time doctrine
    c. airtime doctrine
    d. fairness doctrine

13. The FCC has this many commissioners.
    a. 3
    b. 5
    c. 7
    d. 9

14. The FCC commissioners serve terms for this number of years.
    a. 3   c. 7
    b. 5   d. 9

15. The primary source for national news for most Americans is:
    a. newspapers.   c. radio.
    b. magazines.   d. television.

16. Freedom of the press is protected by the:
    a. First Amendment.   c. Third Amendment.
    b. Second Amendment.   d. Fourth Amendment.

17. The best description of the political status of the airwaves is that it is:
    a. privately owned with no governmental controls.
    b. owned and regulated entirely by the federal or state and local governments.
    c. privately owned but under government supervision.
    d. controlled entirely by one huge corporation.

18. When editors and journalists decide in large measure what American people will know
    about, they are performing the media role of:
    a. gatekeepers.   c. spotlights.
    b. vehicles.   d. talent scouts.

19. The part of government that receives the most press coverage is the:
    a. White House.   c. Supreme Court.
    b. Congress.   d. State and Defense.

20. Televised presidential debates emphasize:
    a. the intellectual content of the candidate's speeches.
    b. the background of the candidate.
    c. the style or image of the candidate.
    d. all of the above

Essay

1. Discuss the developments of newspapers, magazines, radio, and cable services and their impact on America.

2. Describe the constitutional basis of the media and the differences between written media and electronic media.

3. Explain the role of the Federal Communications Commission and its regulations as related to the mass media.

4. In what ways does the mass media make issues and report those issues? Discuss the media as a spotlight and their role as primers.

5. In what ways does the mass media serve as a vehicle of direct communication? Discuss the media as a gatekeeper and the media's influence on political attitudes.

Research Topics and Practical Application

1. Make a list of all of the media outlets in your hometown. Explain the ways these outlets affect your views on local issues and which media source you use for your political information. Discuss why that source is your primary source for information (credibility, visual effects, etc.).

2. Watch an entire news program on a public network channel (ABC, CBS, NBC) and on a cable channel (CNN, FOX). Explain the similarities and differences between the two programs. Discuss which program did a better job of detailing the news and which one had better visual effects.

ANSWER KEY

Completion

1. journalists
2. radio and television
3. telecommunications
4. Fairness Doctrine
5. 1987
6. television
7. leak
8. media
9. fifth branch
10. Shield laws

True-False

1. T
2. F
3. F
4. T
5. T
6. T
7. F
8. T
9. F
10. T

Multiple Choice

1. b
2. a
3. c
4. b
5. c
6. d
7. b
8. a
9. c
10. a
11. d
12. a
13. b
14. c
15. d
16. a
17. c
18. a
19. a
20. c

Chapter 7

INTEREST GROUPS AND POLITICAL PARTIES

CHAPTER REVIEW

Learning Objectives

After studying Chapter 7 you should be able to:

1. Understand why interest groups are important in American politics.

2. Describe the major characteristics of interest groups and analyze how these characteristics relate to the effectiveness of groups.

3. Explain what interest groups do.

4. List and give examples of the major types of interest groups.

5. Evaluate the pros and cons of interest groups as they relate to the ideals of democracy.

6. Explain the purpose and functions of political parties and how they differ from interest groups.

7. Trace the history of the five American party systems and the shifts and realignments that occurred with them.

8. Describe the nature of the two-party system and explain why this type of system developed in the United States.

9. Discuss the formal, electoral, and governmental components of political parties, as well as their significance and functions.

10. Evaluate whether political parties are in a state of decline or resurgence and explain the consequences of each.

11. Comment on the future of the American party system in terms of realignment and resurgence.

Chapter Outline and Summary

I.   Introduction

    A. Group activity is particularly logical in a democracy, where majorities and pluralities rule.

    B. Politics is an arena for group conflict.

    C. Political parties in America perform many vital functions.

II. Interest Groups in American Politics

    A. Introduction

        1. Interest groups are associations of people who hold common views and work to influence what government does.

        2. These groups share the objective of looking out for their members' political interests, but differ in many other ways.

        3. Interest groups are so dominant in America that many see it as a pluralist democracy designed to manage the interplay of group interests. (See "Politics and Ideas: Pluralism and Elitism")

        4. Interest groups are both praised as contributing to democracy and condemned as a threat to the public good.

    B. Characteristics of Interest Groups

        1. Size

            a. Interest groups vary dramatically in size.

            b. Generally, the bigger the group, the more effective it is.

        2. Membership

            a. Groups may have formal or informal membership procedures.

            b. Generally, the stronger the bonds of the members to the group, the more effective it will be.

        3. Organization

            a. Generally, the stronger the group's internal organization, and the more success it has in promoting its interests.

            b. Groups differ in whether they tend to be democratic or autocratic.

        4. Ties to Politics

            a. Interest groups may be essentially nonpolitical (a bowling league), solely political (a political action committee), or have a mixture of political and nonpolitical activities (Roman Catholic Church, National Rifle Association).

5. Agreement with Societal Consensus
    a. Reactionary groups are far to the right.
    b. Radical groups are far to the left.
    c. Groups that stay within the American mainstream are more effective.

C. What Interest Groups Do
    1. Lobbying
        a. The major channel used by interest groups to create public support is the mass media.
        b. Recently, interest groups have used direct mail to get support.
    2. Involvement in the Electoral Process: PACs
        a. Political action committees (PACs) channel money from interest group members to sympathetic political candidates.
        b. Most PACs are multicandidate committees and formally independent of the candidates.
        c. The Federal Election Campaign Finance Reform Act of 1974 spearheaded the proliferation of and contributions to PACs.
        d. PACs have become a controversial issue in American politics.
    3. Involvement in the Legislative Process: Lobbying
        a. Lobbying is the attempt to influence legislation in Congress.
        b. Lobbyists provide information, advice, and testimony to Congress.
        c. Lobbyists are highly paid, respected, and influential.
    4. Involvement in the Administrative and Regulatory Process
        a. Interest groups lobby executive agencies and regulatory commissions representing their interests.
        b. The close ties between interest groups, administrators, and legislators is called the iron triangle.
    5. Involvement in the Judicial Process
        a. Interest groups affect the selection of judges.
        b. Interest groups can file class action suits.
        c. Interest groups can encourage individuals to take legal action.
        d. Interest groups can file *amicus curiae* briefs.

D. Major Interest Groups
    1. Economic Groups
        a. Business advances its interests through groups representing commerce, corporations, and professions.

      b. Labor is primarily represented through unions.

          (i)   The AFL-CIO is an umbrella organization of unions.

          (ii) Labor union influence on the Democratic Party is diminishing.

          (iii) Nonunion workers lack organization and influence.

      c. Although still salient, the power of the agriculture lobby has diminished.

  2. Social Groups

      a. Gender—Women compose one of the largest potential interest groups in the United States.

          (i)   NOW presses for economic and political equality for women.

          (ii) The women's movement is closely tied to politics.

      b. Race—The most prominent biologically based interest group in the United States is the African American population.

          (i)   African Americans pursued their interests through politics, especially through the Democratic Party.

          (ii) The NAACP is the most visible African American interest group.

          (iii) African Americans have increased their voting registration and elective office holders.

  3. Religious Groups

      a. Religious groups, especially the Christian Right, have become active in political issues—especially recently in the abortion controversy.

      b. Most religious groups do not employ registered lobbyists.

  4. Ideological Groups

      a. The ADA espouses a liberal perspective on politics.

  5. Single-Issue Groups

      a. Single-issue groups, such as those in the right-to-life movement, have narrow agendas and limited political goals.

      b. Single-issue groups are controversial to democratic practice.

  6. Public Interest Groups

      a. These groups represent broad notions of the public interest.

      b. Examples include Ralph Nader (consumerism) and Common Cause.

III. Perspectives on Interest Groups

  A. Interest Groups as the Foundation of Democracy

    1. Interest groups promote democracy through competition and representation.

    2. Cross-cutting cleavages stabilize group competition.

    3. Interest Group Elitism

      a.   The structures of interest groups may be undemocratic.

      b.   Big powerful groups dominate small weak ones.

B. Interest Groups Versus the Public Interest

    1. Interest groups are criticized most when seen as using politics to achieve selfish goals.

    2. Many people favor more regulation of interest group activities.

C. Interest Group Gridlock

    1. Too many interest groups, refusing to compromise, can result in interest group gridlock.

IV. Political Parties

A. Introduction

    1. A political party attempts to influence public policy by placing its own members into government positions.

    2. Interest groups and parties are different in that interest groups do not run their own candidates for office but similar in that they both engage in collective political activities.

B. What Parties Do

    1. Parties perform important political socialization functions.
        a. They provide a means for a psychological identification with the world of politics.
        b. They help to structure people's perceptions of politics.
        c. They educate and mobilize people about politics.
        d. They are a major source of political stability.

    2. Parties perform important electoral functions.
        a. They bring diverse political needs together around commonly supported candidates.
        b. They simplify the set of alternatives for voters.
        c. They complement the legal process for choosing public officials.
        d. They recruit and train political leaders.

    3. Parties perform important governmental functions.
        a. They give coherence to public policy.
        b. They help make government more responsive.

V. Basic Characteristics of the American Party System

A. A Two-Party System

    1. Plurality/majority elections encourage a two-party system.

2. Proportional representation, the awarding of legislative seats in proportion to the percentage of votes a party receives, encourages the growth of more than two parties.

3. The cluster of voter opinion toward the ideological center fosters two similar parties trying to attract the same voters.

4. Third parties have forced major parties to address new issues and influenced election results.

B. A Complex Party Structure

    1. Parties and the Levels of Government: National, State, and Local

        a. Party structure parallels the federal system.

        b. The relationship between party levels is not strictly hierarchical.

    2. Parties and Their Components: Formal, Electoral, and Governmental

        a. Formal party organization consists of the people who work for the party.

            (i) At the national level, the party convention chooses the presidential candidate, writes the platform, and designates the national committee.

            (ii) Formerly, state and local political machines used patronage and the spoils system to augment their power.

            (iii) State and local party structure is similar to that of the national parties.

        b. The party in the electorate consists of the citizens who support it.

            (i) Party identification is a psychological attachment to a party by a citizen.

            (ii) A party's coalition consists of the groups of people who support it.

        c. The party in government consists of the people who hold public office.

            (i) Parties in the legislature organize committees and leaders.

            (ii) The executive party and judicial party are informal and less visible.

VI. American Political Parties: Past, Present, and Future

A. Introduction

    1. Although not mentioned in the Constitution, parties do have explicit legal status.

    2. Four specific realignments have created five party systems.

B. Parties Past

    1. The First American Party System (1789–1824): Federalists and Antifederalists

        a. The major issues of this period were centralized versus decentralized power, elite versus open government, government role in the economy, and industrialization versus agriculture.

b. The major parties were the Federalists, dominant until about 1800, and the Antifederalists (Democratic Republicans), who ascended after 1800.

2. The Second American Party System (1824–1860): Democrats and Whigs
   a. By the late 1820s issues of a national bank and states' rights split the Democratic Republican Party, forming the Whig Party (with a vision of a nation modernized by government-backed commerce) and the Democratic Party (with a vision of an agrarian democracy).
   b. Slavery undid the Whig-Democratic party alignment.

3. The Third American Party System (1860–1896): Democrats and Republicans in Close Competition
   a. After the Civil War, the Republican Party established itself as the party of business.
   b. Democrats gained control of the South and re-subjugated African Americans.
   c. Competition characterized this party system and divided congressional and presidential control.

4. The Fourth American Party System (1896–1932): Republican Ascendancy
   a. The 1893 depression sparked the free silver movement led by William Jennings Bryan pitting the Democratic rural, poor, and workers against the Republican urban, industrial, and elite.
   b. Except for the Wilson years, Republicans were dominant until 1929.

C. Parties Present

1. The Fifth American Party System (1932–1968): Democratic Ascendancy
   a. FDR's reaction to the Great Depression issued in an era of social welfare and government direction of the economy.
   b. The Democratic Party remained dominant from 1932–1968.

2. Parties in Decline
   a. In the 1970s and 1980s both national and state party organizations appeared to lose their viability.
   b. At the same time, fewer people identified with a party and the existing coalitions were coming apart.
   c. Through the 1970s and 1980s party discipline and coordination in government seemed to deteriorate.

3. The Causes of Party Decline
   a. Waning patronage and waxing civil service has reduced the parties' power to reward support.
   b. The rise of the mass media has negated candidates' reliance on parties as intermediaries with the public.
   c. PACs and public financing of campaigns have weakened the parties' fundraising activities.

    d.   The rise of primaries weaken the role of party regulars.

    e.   Personal campaign organizations have bypassed traditional party machinery.

    f.   Single-issue interest groups upset the parties' function of coalition-building.

    g.   The rise of the public welfare system reduced citizens' obligation to the party.

    h.   Declining party socialization has reduced people's identification with their parent's political party.

4.   The Consequences of Party Decline

    a.   Citizens are not socialized into politics.

    b.   Electoral alternatives become confusing, creating incoherent policy proposals.

    c.   Interests are not integrated, resulting in fragmentation and paralysis.

    d.   Campaigns and elections become fragmented and personalized.

    e.   Power is not coordinated, resulting in few common bonds of philosophy or loyalty.

    f.   Government is not responsible, so accountability breaks down.

5.   Parties in Resurgence

    a.   Formal Party Organization

       (i)   National party organizations use computers for polling, direct mail, and raising money, especially "soft money."

       (ii) The rejuvenation of party organization started with the Republicans, while the Democrats are trying to catch up.

    b.   The Party in the Electorate

       (i)   Party identification is slowly rising.

       (ii) A reformation of new party coalitions may be occurring.

    c.   The Party in Government

       (i)   Party discipline has not improved.

       (ii) Congressional campaign committees are growing stronger.

6.   Reasons for Party Resurgence

    a.   Parties have adapted to the changing political environment.

    b.   Parties supply candidates with needed resources.

7.   Consequences of Party Resurgence

    a.   Rejuvenated national party organizations may strengthen state and local organizations.

    b.   Strong party organizations may help revive the party in the electorate and the party in the government.

    c.   In a resurgent party system, technology replaces party workers.

D. Parties Future

1.   The Prospects for Realignment

    a.   Some argue that Republican dominance at the presidential level may be solidifying and expanding to other levels.

b. Others argue Republican dominance of the presidency may end as major conservative issues fade.

2. The Future of Resurgence

a. Recent changes in the party system may mark a broad and permanent change based on centralization, the importance of the media, and the demand for campaign money.

b. Parties have shown the ability to adapt to changing circumstances, eventually and sufficiently.

VII. Summary

Key Terms, Concepts, and Personalities

After studying Chapter 7 you should be able to identify and describe the significance of:

amicus curiae brief
caucus
Christian Right
class action suit
coalition
cross-cutting cleavage
dealignment
decline
direct mail
electoral functions
formal party organization
governmental functions
grass-roots lobbying
interest group elitism
iron triangle
lobbying
majority election
melting pot

movement
national committee
national convention
party in government
party system
platform
pluralist democracy
plurality election
political machine
political party
proportional representation
realignment
resurgence
runoff election
single-member district
socialization functions
state committee
third party

TESTING YOUR UNDERSTANDING

Completion

1. James Madison wrote in _____ about the dangers of factions.

2. PACs blossomed into prominence as a result of the _____
_____ _____ _____
_____ _____.

3. Interest groups, legislators, and administrators are sometimes called the
_____ _____ of American politics.

4. Interest groups have brought cases before the courts through _____
_____ _____ representing a large number of
individuals with the same grievance.

5. America has been known as the _____ _____ society
because it consists of people of all races and nationalities.

6. No issue in recent years has drawn religious groups more into the political fray than
_____.

7. The tendency for different coalitions to form on different issues is called a
_____ _____.

8. When an overabundance of interest groups refusing to compromise develops, the situation
is called an interest group _____.

9. One of the _____ functions of parties is to educate citizens and mobilize
them into political action.

10. A change in party systems occurs after a short period of political turmoil and change is
called _____.

11. In the second American party system, the spiritual descendants of the Federalist Party was
the _____ Party.

12. One of the major reasons why the United States has a two-party system is because of the
system of _____ elections.

13. A statement of a political party's proposed program is called its _____.

14. All of the groups of people who together make up the main supporters of a particular party are called the party's _____.

15. The increase in party identification since 1978 has primarily benefited the _____ Party.

Compare and Contrast

1. elitism and pluralism

2. Federal Election Campaign Act of 1974 and McCain-Feingold

3. class action suits and *amicus curiae* brief

4. Chamber of Commerce and grass-roots lobbying

5. National Organization for Women and National Association for the Advancement of Colored People

6. political party and interest group

7. socialization, electoral, and governmental functions

8. Federalists and Antifederalists

9. plurality election, majority election, and proportional representation

10. formal party organization, party in the electorate, and party in the government

11. national convention, national committee

12. political machine, patronage

13. decline and resurgence

True-False

1. Groups that stay within the political mainstream tend to be more influential. T F

2. Most PACs are registered with the Federal Election Commission. T F

3. PACs are especially significant at the national level for presidential campaigns. T F

4. The influence of agricultural organizations have been on the rise since the Reagan Administration. T F

5. Less than two percent of the African American population belongs to the NAACP. T F

6. The influence of the Christian Right declined dramatically in the late 1980s. T F

7. When parties recruit and train political leaders they are performing one of their electoral functions. T F

8. Political parties are formally sanctioned in Article III, Section 4 of the Constitution. T F

9. The Democratic Party was the first truly national political party. T F

10. A system of proportional representation encourages the development of a two-party system. T F

11. Third parties have had very little influence on the American political system. T F

12. The relationship between the national, state, and local party organizations follows a strict hierarchical pattern. T F

13. Throughout the 1970s and 1980s party discipline and coordination seemed to deteriorate. T F

14. The increase in the number of single-issue interest groups has contributed to the resurgence of political parties based on new coalitions. T F

15. The political parties have shown a keen ability to eventually adapt to changing circumstances. T F

Multiple Choice

1. The theory that sees power as dispersed among many different centers of power is called:
   a. elitism.
   b. pluralism.
   c. democracy.
   d. communism.

2. The more politically influential groups in America tend to be:
   a. reactionary.
   b. radical.
   c. mainstream.
   d. nonideological.

3. The major means by which interest groups try to create public support or sympathy for their political goals is:
   a. the mass media.
   b. direct mail.
   c. opinion leaders.
   d. political action committees.

4. The McCain-Feingold legislation set the limit on individual contributions to candidates at:
   a. $2,000.
   b. $4,000.
   c. $5,000.
   d. $10,000.

5. Lobbyists:
   a. are not a reliable source of information.
   b. cannot by law testify before congressional committees.
   c. tend to be shady figures and shunned by Washington society.
   d. are important channels by which PAC money gets to legislators.

6. The iron triangle of American politics consists of:
   a. interest group representatives, legislators, and judges.
   b. congress, the presidency, and the supreme court.
   c. interest group representatives, legislators, and administrators.
   d. interest group representatives, PACs, and political candidates.

7. Regarding the judicial process, interest groups:
   a. have little influence over the selection of judges.
   b. use class action suits to further their causes.
   c. are not permitted by law to mail information to judges.
   d. all of the above

8. The American Federation of Labor-Congress of Industrial Organizations:
   a. has increased its membership over the past decade.
   b. no longer supports the Democratic Party.
   c. spearheads political activity on behalf of organized labor.
   d. has tight control of its rank-and-file members.

9. Which of the following statements about the National Organization for Women is false?
   a. It supports freedom of choice on abortion.
   b. It is not actively involved in electoral politics.
   c. It has only about 160,000 members.
   d. It is the most prominent women's political organization.

10. Most African Americans:
    a. support the Democratic Party.
    b. support the Republican Party.
    c. are members of the NAACP.
    d. are apolitical.

11. In recent years the most important political issue concerning religious groups has been:
    a. the Middle East conflict.   c. school prayer.
    b. abortion.   d. poverty.

12. Americans for Democratic Action is a(n):
    a political action committee for the Democratic Party.
    b. single-issue group.
    c. public interest group.
    d. ideological group.

13. An example of a single-issue group would be the:
    a. National Right-to-Life Committee.
    b. National Organization of Women.
    c. Americans for Democratic Action.
    d. NAACP.

14. A factor that helps contribute to stability in the American system of interest group politics is:
    a. interest group gridlock.   c. cross-cutting cleavages.
    b. iron law of oligarchy.   d. interest group elitism.

15. When a pluralistic system becomes paralyzed because too many interest groups refuse to compromise is known as:
    a. interest group gridlock.
    b. interest group anarchy.
    c. interest group elitism.
    d. interest group cleavage.

16. The main difference between interest groups and political parties is that:
    a. political parties do not have formal membership.
    b. interest groups do not engage in collective political activities.
    c. interest groups do not run candidates for public office.
    d. political parties do not attempt to influence public opinion.

17. All of the following are socialization functions of political parties except:
    a. providing a psychological hook that pulls people into politics.
    b. giving coherence to governmental policy.
    c. structuring people's perceptions of politics.
    d. providing a source of political stability.

18. All of the following are electoral functions of political parties except:
    a. simplifying the set of alternatives.
    b. educating citizens and mobilizing them into political action.
    c. complementing the established process for choosing leaders.
    d. providing a means for recruiting and training political leaders.

19. Each party system that evolved from its predecessor in a relatively short period of political turmoil and change is called:
    a. factionalization.
    b. dealignment.
    c. realignment.
    d. anarchy.

20. The first truly national political party was the:
    a. Federalist Party.
    b. Whig Party.
    c. Republican Party.
    d. Democratic Party.

21. The underlying cause for the shift from the fourth to the fifth American party system was:
    a. the civil war.
    b. Watergate.
    c. the Great Depression.
    d. the free silver movement.

22. Since 1968 the most dramatic shift in voting patterns has been in the:
    a. Northeast.
    b. Midwest.
    c. West.
    d. South.

23. A multiparty system is most likely to occur when the electoral system is based on:
    a. plurality.
    b. majority.
    c. runoffs.
    d. proportional representation.

24. Third parties in the American political system:
    a. are never taken seriously.
    b. have forced the major parties to address important issues.
    c. have never influenced the outcome of a presidential election.
    d. often have pivotal voting power in Congress.

25. All of the following activities occur at the party's national convention except:
    a. choosing the party's congressional leaders.
    b. writing the party's platform.
    c. selecting the party's candidates for president and vice-president.
    d. formally designating the national committee.

26. Which of the following statements about the party in the electorate is false?
    a. Party identification is based on psychological identification.
    b. The party in the electorate is defined by people saying they think of themselves as belonging to a party.
    c. Various groups in society come together to form a party's coalition.
    d. Party identification is very stable over time.

27. Part of the evidence that political parties were in decline by the 1970s and 1980s includes:
    a. a decrease in the percentage of people who identified with a political party.
    b. an increase in the number of people voting for third parties.
    c. a resurgence of political machines at the state level.
    d. a shift in voting that brought more African Americans and poor people to the Republican Party.

28. Which of the following is considered a cause of party decline?
    a. The increased use of political patronage.
    b. The rise of the public welfare system.
    c. The inability of parties and candidates to master the mass media.
    d. The increased use of caucuses to choose candidates.

29. Which of the following is not a consequence of party decline?
    a. Citizens are not socialized into politics.
    b. Electoral alternatives become confusing.
    c. Campaigns and elections become fragmented.
    d. Power becomes more centralized.

30. Evidence that the party in government is in resurgence includes the fact that:
    a. party discipline in Congress has strengthened.
    b. coordination between the president and his party in Congress has improved.
    c. congressional campaign committees have been strengthened.
    d. all of the above

Essay

1. Explain what factors influence the effectiveness of an interest group. Write a profile of the characteristics of an ideal interest group in terms of effectiveness.

2. What is a Political Action Committee (PAC)? Why has the number of PACs increased so rapidly since 1974? In your opinion, are PACs an asset or a liability to American politics?

3. In what ways are interest groups involved in each of the three branches of government? Where do you believe they have the most influence and why? What is meant by the iron triangle of American politics?

4. List and summarize the six major types of interest groups and give examples of each type or category.

5. In what ways might it be said that interest groups weaken and strengthen democracy?

6. Answer the questions posed in the text: What is a political party? What do parties do? In your answer be sure to compare political parties to interest groups and explain the various functions performed by political parties.

7. Explain why the United States developed into a two-party system while other democratic countries have multi-party systems.

8. If political parties are in decline, what factors have caused this decline?

9. Present an argument supporting the statement that the American political parties are in a period of resurgence.

Research Topics and Practical Application

1. Go to the library and browse through a copy of the *Encyclopedia of Associations* to get a feel for the extent of interest group activity in the United States. Make a list of several examples of groups in each of the six categories of interest groups described in the text. Collect data for each organization on its membership, number of staff, age of the organization, location of its headquarters, and publications. Make a table that compares these data according to the categories of interest groups. Do any patterns emerge? How do the different categories of interest groups differ? How are they similar?

2. Write a case study of a specific interest group. Choose one that is of particular interest to you. Contact the group to get current information. Describe the group in terms of its size, membership, and organization. What are the policy goals of the group and what strategies has it used to achieve these goals? To what extent is the group involved in politics? Has it ever lobbied for particular legislation? Does it have a political action committee? If so, who does the PAC contribute to and how much has it contributed?

3. Political party platforms represent the best available statements of the party's and presidential candidate's positions on important policy issues. Find copies of the Democratic and Republican platforms for the 2008 election in your school library. Using these documents compare and contrast the two parties on the basis of ideology and coalition-building. In terms of ideology summarize each party's basic positions on issues in the areas of foreign, economic, and social policy. Where do they agree and disagree and what philosophical or ideological patterns seem to emerge? Make a list of the groups of people that the platform seems to be attempting to appeal to. Some of these groups may be apparent on the basis of the policy and position addressed. Is there a pattern in the type of groups that each party tries to appeal to most? What do your findings tell us about the possibility of realignment?

ANSWER KEY

Completion

1. *Federalist No. 10*
2. Federal Election Campaign Act of 1974
3. iron triangle
4. class action suits
5. melting pot
6. abortion
7. cross-cutting cleavage
8. gridlock
9. socialization
10. realignment
11. Whig
12. plurality
13. platform
14. coalition
15. Republican

True-False

1. T
2. T
3. F
4. F
5. T
6. T
7. T
8. F
9. T
10. F
11. F
12. F
13. T
14. F
15. T

Multiple Choice

1. b
2. c
3. a
4. a
5. d
6. c
7. b
8. c
9. b
10. a
11. b
12. d
13. a
14. c
15. a

16. c
17. b
18. b
19. c
20. d
21. c
22. d
23. d
24. b
25. a
26. d
27. a
28. b
29. d
30. c

Chapter 8

CAMPAIGNS AND ELECTIONS

CHAPTER REVIEW

Learning Objectives

After studying Chapter 8 you should be able to:

1. Explain the factors that have an influence on whether citizens in the United States vote or do not vote, noting how the franchise has been expanded through the years.

2. Compare and contrast the factors that influence who voters vote for.

3. Present a profile of the typical candidate for president and describe the factors that influence a candidate's decision to run.

4. Explain the impact of the media and money on presidential campaigns.

5. Outline the process for getting nominated, choosing a running mate, and getting elected president of the United States.

6. Evaluate the various proposals to reform elections.

7. Discuss the important aspects of congressional elections and how running for Congress is different from running for president.

Chapter Outline and Summary

I. Introduction

    A. An election campaign is a complex event involving many actors.

II. The Voter's Perspective: To Vote or Not to Vote

    A. Introduction

        1. Interest in politics becomes aroused around election day.
        2. Few Americans become involved in campaigns beyond casual interest and discussions.
        3. Voting is the most frequent and meaningful act of political participation.

B. Voting Requirements and Eligibility

    1. Race

        a. The Fifteenth Amendment granted voting rights to African Americans.

        b. Jim Crow laws, such as the literacy test, poll tax, and white primary denied African Americans the right to vote in the South.

        c. These barriers were eliminated by constitutional amendments, Supreme Court decisions, and legislative acts.

    2. Sex prohibitions to voting were eliminated by the Nineteenth Amendment, which granted female suffrage.

    3. The voting age was reduced from 21 to 18 by the Twenty-sixth Amendment.

    4. Other voting restrictions involve noncitizens, felons, mental patients, and residency requirements (now limited to 30 days).

    5. Registration

        a. Mail and election day registration increases turnout.

        b. Democrats tend to favor easier registration, while Republicans oppose it.

        c. Originally, registration was intended to prevent voter fraud.

C. Who Votes?

    1. Social Characteristics

        a. There is now a general convergence in voting rates among various types of citizens.

        b. Older people, more educated people, and people with higher incomes are all more likely to vote. (See "Politics and Economics: Turnout, Choice, and Economic Status.")

    2. Psychological Influences

        a. The greater a person's interest in politics and sense of political efficacy, the more likely that person will vote.

        b. The stronger a person's attachment to a political party, the more likely that person will vote.

    3. Offices and Elections

        a. Turnout is high for high-stimulus elections and low for low-stimulus elections.

D. Declining Turnout

    1. Voting turnout has varied since the late nineteenth century and is now at one of its lowest points.

    2. Decline in turnout has been attributed to registration and voting procedures, political alienation, decreasing partisanship, and low political efficacy.

3. Whether low voter turnout is bad or indifferent for democracy has been a matter of debate. (See "Contemporary Controversies, Low Voter Turnout: A Comparative Perspective.")

III. The Voter's Perspective: How to Vote

A. Parties

1. For many years, affiliation with a political party was the mainstay of voting decisions.

2. While the role of the party has weakened, strong party identifiers remain loyal and consistent in their voting.

B. Candidates

1. Opinions about candidates themselves play a powerful role in influencing voters.

2. Voters emphasize political experience, effective leadership, and attractive personal qualities.

C. Issues

1. Issues tend to affect voting choice more than ever before.

2. Economic issues, especially personal well-being, greatly affect voting choice.

3. Ideology also has some effect on voting choice.

D. Conclusion

1. The relation between parties, issues, and candidates as influences on the vote in presidential elections is complex.

IV. The Candidate's Perspective: Running for President

A. Who Runs for President?

1. Constitutional qualifications include natural-born citizenship, 14-year residency, at least 35 years old, and limited to two terms (Twenty-second Amendment).

2. Other factors include experience in a high political office, being an incumbent, being on the successful side of mainstream America, having a clean personal and political reputation, having an attractive image, and—most importantly—determination.

B. The Media Campaign

1. Candidates' principal concern now is mobilizing the media.

2. Free television time is gained through the use of interviews and short "sound bites."

3. Candidates have come to rely on professional media consultants to plan campaign strategy.

4. The media increasingly focus on opinion polls and the horse race aspects of the campaign.

C. Campaign Finance

1. The Federal Election Campaign Act (FECA) requires disclosure of sources of funding and puts limits on campaign contributions and candidate spending.

2. The Revenue Act of 1971 allows taxpayers to contribute to the Presidential Election Campaign Fund.

3. Major-party candidates can opt for federal financing if they refuse public contributions after the convention.

4. The soft money loophole provided a means to raise unlimited amounts of money at the state and local level that can indirectly be used for the presidential campaign.

5. The McCain-Feingold legislation banned soft money and restricted issue ads.

6. Independent "527s" are now a current loophole to McCain-Feingold that have a similar effect as soft money.

D. Getting Nominated

1. Party caucuses have recently gained in importance, particularly the early Iowa caucus.

2. Primary elections are intraparty elections that select party nominees for the general election.

   a. An open primary allows any voter regardless of party affiliation to vote in a particular party's primary.

   b. A closed primary allows only registered party voters to vote for candidates of that party.

   c. The earliest presidential primaries are the most important in sorting out potential candidates.

3. The party conventions select party nominees, draft rules, and write the party platform.

4. Choosing a Running Mate

   a. The vice-presidential nominee is usually chosen to balance the ticket.

   b. The choice of a running mate is made by the presidential candidate.

   c. The vice-president is less an object of scorn as in the past.

   d. The vice-presidency is the most direct path to the presidency.

     5. Getting Elected

        a. The president is elected indirectly through the Electoral College, in which each state has electors equal to the number of representatives and senators from that state, thus setting the stage for an emphasis on large states in the campaign.

        b. Candidates seek to instill an image in the minds of the voters, with incumbents having a distinct advantage.

        c. Candidates must decide on whether to confront or evade issues.

        d. Debates are risky for an incumbent, but can be the best strategic opportunity for a challenger.

        e. Campaign strategy is at the mercy of events that can make a candidate look either inept or "presidential."

E. The Electoral College

     1. The number of electors for each state is equal to its U.S. congressional representation (i.e., number of representatives plus senators).

     2. A faithless elector is an individual who votes for someone other than who they were committed to vote for.

     3. An individual wins the presidential election by winning the majority in the Electoral College (not necessarily winning a plurality in the popular vote).

     4. Because of the potential for a popular vote minority president, there have been proposals to reform the electoral system:

        a. Replacing the Electoral College with a direct popular election of the president or using the congressional district winner system.

        b. Changing the two-term limit placed on presidents.

F. Campaign Strategies

     1. Challengers want to debate; incumbents see no advantage in debating.

     2. Sometimes outside events can impact negatively on a president.

V. The Candidate's Perspective: Running for Congress

A. Campaign Finance

     1. House and Senate elections have become very expensive.

     2. There is no public financing for congressional campaigns.

     3. Congressional elections have seen efforts to get around restrictions imposed by federal campaign finance laws.

     4. Money helps challengers more than officeholders.

B. Incumbency

    1. Incumbency is even more an asset to members of Congress, especially in the House, than it is to presidents.

    2. Five out of six congressional districts are safe seats.

    3. Incumbents are better known, can take credit, can raise money easier, and can use the resources of their offices to get reelected.

C. Parties, Candidates, and Issues

    1. After incumbency, the single most important determinant of voting in congressional elections is party.

    2. Except for the economy, issues are of little importance in congressional elections due to the lack of information.

    3. Candidates for the House are judged on the qualities of trust and competence while Senate candidates are judged in terms of experience and ability.

    4. Presidential Popularity

        a. When congressional elections coincide with a presidential election, a presidential candidate whose popularity helps his party's congressional candidates is said to have coattails.

        b. In midterm elections, the congressional vote may be interpreted as a referendum on the president.

        c. The president's party historically loses seats in midterm elections.

VI. Summary

Key Terms, Concepts, and Personalities

After studying Chapter 8 you should be able to identify and describe the significance of:

balance the ticket	Federal Election Campaign Act of 1974
blanket primary	franking privilege
caucus	general election
closed primary	grandfather clause
coattails	literacy test
congressional districting system	McCain-Feingold
direct popular election	media consultant
Electoral College	Nineteenth Amendment
exit poll	open primary
faithless elector	party convention
political action committee (PAC)	Super Tuesday

poll tax
Presidential Election Campaign Fund
primary election
regional primary
register
residence requirements
safe seat
soft money

term limits
Twenty-fourth Amendment
Twenty-second Amendment
Twenty-sixth Amendment
Twenty-third Amendment
unit rule system
Voting Rights Act of 1965
Voting Rights Act of 1970

TESTING YOUR UNDERSTANDING

Completion

1. In most places in the United States, potential voters are required to
_____ before they are allowed to vote.

2. Two social characteristics that show the strongest relation to voting turnout are
_____ and _____.

3. The three major factors that seem most to influence how people vote are
_____, _____, and _____.

4. The three virtues that voters seem to consider most important in a candidate are attractive
personal qualities, _____, and _____.

5. The most important quality to be a presidential contender is _____.

6. Today, presidential candidates tend to rely on more professional _____
_____ to plan and execute their campaign strategy.

7. A major criticism of the media is their tendency to focus on the _____
_____ aspects of the presidential campaign at the expense of the issues.

8. Soft money contributions were banned with passage of the _____
legislation.

9. A House district where party affiliation is so lopsided that one or the other party is assured victory is called a _____ _____.

10. A presidential candidate whose popularity appears to give a boost to his party's candidates for the House and Senate is said to have _____.

Compare and Contrast

1. literacy test, poll tax, grandfather clause, and white primary

2. Fifteenth Amendment, Nineteenth Amendment, and Twenty-sixth Amendment

3. high-stimulus elections and low-stimulus elections

4. Federal Election Campaign Act and Presidential Campaign Fund

5. caucus, primary elections, and general election

6. open primary and closed primary

True-False

1. Studies have shown that younger people are more likely to vote than older people. T F

2. Increasing political alienation or distrust has been shown to be the primary reason for low voter turnout in the United States. T F

3. In recent years, political party affiliation has become a less important determinant of voting decisions. T F

4. The best assurance of being elected president is already to be president. T F

5. Candidates tend to favor long television advertisements in order to maximize public exposure and issue formulation. T F

6. The Federal Election Campaign Act of 1974 requires the full disclosure of the sources and uses of presidential campaign funds. T F

7. An incumbent president has little to gain in accepting a debate with his opponent. T F

8. The Electoral College results in small states being represented out of proportion to their populations. T F

9. Candidates for the House and Senate receive significant amounts of public financing, for their campaigns. T F

10. Presidential electors for the Electoral College must vote for the candidate they are committed to. T F

Multiple Choice

1. Women were given the right to vote by the:
   a. Fifteenth Amendment.
   b. Nineteenth Amendment.
   c. Twenty-second Amendment.
   d. Twenty-sixth Amendment.

2. The two social characteristics that show the strongest relation to voting are:
   a. party identification and income.
   b. race and religion.
   c. age and education.
   d. sex and regional habitat.

3. Each of the following may be considered a reason for declining voter turnout except:
   a. increasing political alienation and distrust.
   b. an increase in the number of younger citizens of voting age.
   c. decreasing partisanship.
   d. declining sense of external political efficacy.

4. Voters tend to prefer presidential candidates with:
   a. experience.
   b. leadership qualities.
   c. attractive personal qualities.
   d. all of the above

5. The mainspring issue driving most electoral decisions seems to be:
   a. foreign policy issues.
   b. economic issues.
   c. social issues.
   d. civil rights issues.

6. In recent years, serious contenders for the presidency:
   a. have most often come from the successful side of mainstream America.
   b. usually come from the House of Representatives.
   c. have never, until George Bush, served as vice-president.
   d. have rarely had college educations.

7. In recent years, the media campaign for presidential elections has:
   a. emphasized long televised speeches that focus on in-depth discussions of public policy.
   b. focused on making a positive point about one's own candidacy.
   c. been devoted to short television advertisements that focus on simple images and issues.
   d. been de-emphasized in favor of more personal appearances.

8. The Federal Election Campaign Act:
   a. created a system of public financing for presidential campaigns through the federal income tax system.
   b. limited the amount of money a PAC can contribute to all federal candidates.
   c. required all contributions to be funneled through the state and local political party.
   d. required full disclosure of sources and uses of campaign funds.

9. "Soft money" refers to money:
   a. provided for presidential campaigns through federal funds.
   b. raised by state and local parties for certain activities without any restrictions.
   c. contributed to a campaign by a Political Action Committee.
   d. raised by taxpayers by earmarking $1 of federal income tax for the Presidential Campaign fund.

10. The most common method by which political parties choose presidential electors in the states is through a:
    a. caucus.
    b. general election.
    c. open primary.
    d. closed primary.

11. The choice of a running mate is usually made:
    a. long before the party convention.
    b. by the rules committee at the party convention.
    c. to balance the ticket geographically or ideologically.
    d. on the basis of ideological and policy agreement with the presidential candidate.

12. Presidential debates:
    a. are most advantageous for challengers.
    b. are required by law before a candidate can receive federal funds.
    c. have had little impact on the outcome of presidential elections.
    d. all of the above

13. After incumbency, the single most important determinant of voting in congressional races is:
   a. party.
   b. issues.
   c. media exposure.
   d. the candidates themselves.

14. Midterm congressional elections:
   a. usually result in a gain for the president's party.
   b. are often viewed as a referendum on how the president is doing.
   c. usually result in high voter turnout.
   d. have historically favored the Republican Party.

15. McCain-Feingold:
   a. limited individual campaign contributions to $1,000.
   b. limited PAC campaign contributions to $2,000.
   c. outlawed soft money campaign contributions.
   d. outlawed hard money campaign contributions.

Essay

1. Describe how the franchise has been expanded, especially in terms of race, sex, and age. How has expansion of the franchise affected voter turnout?

2. Explain how political parties, candidates, and issues influence how people vote.

3. Explain the importance of the media in presidential election campaigns, especially the effect of television, media consultants, negative campaigning, and opinion polls. What proposals have been suggested to reform the roll of the media in presidential campaigns?

4. What is the importance of money in a campaign? Explain how campaign financing is regulated. What further proposals have been made to reform campaign financing?

5. How does incumbency affect presidential and congressional elections? What advantages do incumbents have, particularly in congressional elections?

Research Topics and Practical Applications

1. Find voter turnout statistics for the 2008 presidential election and the 2006 congressional election for your home congressional district and state. Compare these figures to the national average voter turnout in these two elections. Explain the differences in these statistics in terms of the factors suggested in the text as influencing voter turnout, such as the social and economic characteristics of your congressional district, the type of election, and the degree of electoral competition.

2. Write a brief biographical sketch of each of the two major party candidates for president since Roosevelt. Include in your sketch information on the candidates' former employment (especially elected offices), education, religion, income, wealth and any other personal qualities you may think of. What patterns are apparent? Are there any obvious differences between winners and losers? What are the implications of your findings for democratic governance?

ANSWER KEY

Completion

1. register
2. age, education
3. parties, candidates, issues
4. experience, leadership
5. determination
6. campaign consultants
7. horse race
8. McCain-Feingold
9. safe seat
10. coattails

True-False

1. F
2. F
3. T
4. T
5. F
6. T
7. T
8. T
9. F
10. F

Multiple Choice

1. b
2. c
3. a
4. d
5. b
6. a
7. c
8. d
9. b
10. d
11. c
12. a
13. a
14. b
15. c

Chapter 9

CONGRESS

CHAPTER REVIEW

Learning Objectives

After studying Chapter 9 you should be able to:

1. Detail the constitutional powers of Congress.

2. Describe the members of Congress in terms of their characteristics, roles, work responsibilities, and legislative norms.

3. Explain how Congress is organized, particularly in terms of party leadership, the committee system, and congressional staff.

4. Outline the stages and procedures relating to how a bill becomes a law.

5. Explain the political interaction between Congress, the president, lobbies, and the bureaucracy.

6. Comment on the future roles of a changing Congress.

Chapter Outline and Summary

I. Introduction

   A. Congress is the branch of government that is most responsive and representative of the American people.

II. The Constitutional Powers of Congress

   A. Introduction

      1. The Constitution enumerates certain powers to Congress and implies others through the necessary and proper clause.

2. Constitutional constraints on Congress include restrictions on enumerated and implied powers and specific limitations such as bans on bills of attainder and ex post facto laws.

3. The Constitution requires Congress to share many of its powers.

    a. Congress shares powers with the president and Supreme Court through the system of checks and balances.

    b. Congress shares powers within itself, between the House of Representatives and Senate.

        (i) The House was designed to be more representative and thus impulsive.

        (ii) Until the Seventeenth Amendment, the Senate was indirectly elected and designed to be more deliberative.

    c. Many differences remain between the House and Senate. (See Table 9.1.)

4. The House has had problems with malapportionment (districts of unequal population size—declared unconstitutional) and gerrymandering (districts of unusual shapes or sizes—irregularly drawn districts must meet constitutional muster).

III. The Members of Congress

   A. Who Are They?

      1. Constitutional requirements for membership in Congress include very few restrictions.

      2. Members are primarily white, upper-middle-class, and male.

   B. How Do They See Their Role?

      1. Trustees follow their own judgment (28% of members).

      2. Delegates vote their constituents' desires (23% of members).

      3. Politicos combine both roles (46% of members).

   C. How Long Do They Stay?

      1. In the 1800s members of Congress served fewer terms.

      2. Between 1850 and 1950 the average tenure increased and the percentage of first-term members declined.

      3. In the 1970s these trends flattened.

D. How Much Do They Do?

1. In the nineteenth and early twentieth centuries the workload in Congress was light and needed less time.

2. Today, the business of Congress has expanded in both volume and complexity, requiring full attention.

E. What Do They Do?

1. Due to the need for reelection, members must see to the desires of their district or state through constant communication and pork-barrel politics.

2. A member is expected to serve as an ombudsman to help with casework on behalf of individual constituents.

F. How Do They See Each Other?

1. Legislative norms are standards of behavior in Congress.
   a. Members are expected to practice reciprocity or logrolling.
   b. Members are expected to be courteous to each other.
   c. Members are expected to specialize in one or two subjects.

2. The period of apprenticeship for new members of Congress has become an outmoded tradition for the most part.

IV. The Structure of Congress

A. Party Leadership: The House

1. The Speaker of the House is its presiding officer.
   a. The Speaker is next in line to succeed the president after the vice-president.
   b. The Speaker is nominated by the majority party.
   c. The Speaker's power reached its pinnacle under Joseph Cannon, but a House revolt in 1911 took most of the Speaker's powers.
   d. In 1975 House Democrats increased the substantive powers of the Speaker by making him or her the chair of the Steering and Policy Committee, with the power to nominate all Democratic members to the Rules Committee.

2. The majority leader is the Speaker's chief deputy and the second most powerful figure in the majority party.

3. The leader of the loyal opposition is the minority leader.

4. The party whip acts as an assistant majority or minority leader and is the heart of the party communication system.

B. Party Leadership: The Senate

1. The roles of president of the Senate (vice-president) and president pro tempore are primarily ceremonial and honorific.

2. The majority leader is the dominant figure in the Senate.

   a. The majority leader controls debate on the floor and influences committee assignments.

   b. Senators are more independent and harder to lead than members of the House.

   c. Party leaders are media personalities and spokespersons for their party.

3. Senate whips basically serve floor leaders as vote counters.

C. The Committee System

1. Standing committees approve legislation for floor debate.

2. Joint committees are permanent committees made up of members from both houses.

3. Special or select committees are created periodically to study particular problems or new areas of legislation.

4. Congressional seniority and committee seniority are based on length of service and affect privileges granted to members.

5. Committee assignments are made by party leaders and caucuses.

   a. Members concerned with reelection seek committees with direct impact on their constituents.

   b. Members interested in influencing policy seek committees concerned with broad public issues.

   c. Members who want to expand their influence seek committees that deal with matters important to all members.

   d. The attraction of certain committees changes with time.

   e. Members must actively lobby to get the assignments they want.

6. Once all powerful, committee chairs lost much of their power in the reforms of the 1970s.

D. Subcommittees

1. Standing committees are usually divided into subcommittees.

2. Subcommittees have gained legislative independence and power in the House (subcommittee government), but less in the Senate.

3. The rise of subcommittee government has made coalition-building and compromise more difficult.

E. Congressional Staff and Agencies

    1. The increasing number of congressional staff members reflects the complexity of modern government.

    2. A typical congressional office will include a legislative assistant, administrative assistant, caseworkers, press aide, and others.

    3. Staff members are usually young, well educated, and male.

    4. Committee staffers are responsible for developing legislation that comes from the committees.

    5. Members have become increasingly dependent on their staffs.

    6. Agencies that provide Congress with policy research and analysis include the Congressional Research Service, Government Accountability Office, and the Congressional Budget Office.

V. Congressional Procedures: How a Bill Becomes a Law

A. Committee to Floor Debate

    1. After a member introduces a bill it is sent to the appropriate committee and subcommittee for study and public hearings.

    2. After hearings, the bill is marked up (given precise language and amendments).

    3. If approved, the bill goes to the respective chamber.

B. Floor Debate: The House

    1. Bills reported out of committee are listed on a House calendar (Union, House, Private or Consent Calendar).

    2. The Speaker and majority leader determine which bills are called off the calendar and placed on the floor. Minor bills may be sent directly to the floor by a suspension of the rules.

    3. Most major bills go to the Rules Committee where a closed, open, or modified rule is given.

    4. Floor debate follows specific rules and may be conducted in the Committee of the Whole.

    5. Floor debate is followed by amendments (which must be germane to the bill) and electronic voting.

C. Floor Debate: The Senate

    1. Senate procedures are more flexible with only two calendars (Executive Calendar and Calendar of General Orders) and no restrictions on debate and amendments.

    2. Riders (nongermane amendments) that would otherwise be killed are often put on more popular bills.

    3. Unanimous consent agreements limit the terms of Senate debates.

    4. A filibuster (talking a bill to death) can be stopped by cloture whereby a three-fifths vote ends debate. (See "Politics and Ideas: Two Ideologues in the Senate.")

D. The Conference Committee: Resolving Senate-House Differences

    1. When major differences exist in a bill, a House-Senate Conference Committee must reconcile them.

    2. The conference often requires hard bargaining and compromise.

    3. Once finished, the conference compromise bill is sent back to the House and Senate for approval.

VI. Congress and the Political System

A. Lobbies

    1. Although criticized for involvement in scandals, lobbyists foster dialogue between the people and Congress.

    2. Lobbyists are most successful in affecting distributive policies and least successful with redistributive policies.

    3. Lobbyists often utilize public opinion to affect laws.

    4. Informal legislative caucuses have strong ties to interest groups (such as the textile caucus and steel caucus).

B. The Bureaucracy

    1. Along with interest groups and congressional committees, bureaucratic agencies often develop informal partnerships, called subgovernments or iron triangles, to influence distributive policy.

    2. The effectiveness of iron triangles has declined as a result of aggressive media and public interest groups.

VII. What Role for a Changing Congress

    A. Congress has democratized its rules and opened up its procedures.

    B. Since Vietnam, Congress has challenged presidential control of policy by altering presidential proposals and initiating major reforms.

    C. Although Congress cannot lead the nation, like the president, it does reflect the democratic process.

VIII. Summary

Key Terms, Concepts, and Personalities

After studying Chapter 9 you should be able to identify and describe the significance of:

administrative assistant

calendar

casework

checks and balances

closed rule

cloture

Committee of the Whole

congressional seniority

delegate role

distributive policies

filibuster

gerrymandering

House-Senate Conference Committee

joint committees

legislative assistant

legislative norms

majority leader (House)

majority leader (Senate)

malapportionment

mark-up

minority leader (House)

minority leader (Senate)

modified rule

necessary and proper clause

open rule

party whip

pork barrel politics

president pro tempore

reciprocity (or logrolling)

redistributive policies

riders

Rules Committee

Seventeenth Amendment

Speaker of the House

special or select committees

standing committees

trustee role

unanimous consent agreements

TESTING YOUR UNDERSTANDING

Completion

1. Members of Congress who primarily vote according to their constituents' desires follow the _____ role of representation.

2. When members of Congress intervene with the federal bureaucracy on behalf of individual constituents they are serving as _____.

3. The _____ Committee clears all major legislation going to the floor of the House.

4. Congressional _____ can affect committee assignments, office space, and even deference shown to a member on the floor.

5. The agency that reports to Congress on the efficiency and performance of federal programs is called the _____ _____ _____.

6. When a subcommittee decides on a bill's precise language and amendments, the bill is said to be _____ _____.

7. The strategy in the Senate where continuing debate is used to prevent passage of a bill is called the _____.

8. The informal partnerships between interest groups, congressional committees, and bureaucratic agencies are called _____ _____.

9. The _____ provided for the direct election of U.S. Senators in 1913.

10. _____ is the congressional task of handling requests by constituents for information or assistance with the federal bureaucracy.

Compare and Contrast

1. bill of attainder and ex post facto laws

2. trustee role, delegate role, and politico style

3. House and Senate majority and minority leaders

4. Steering and Policy Committee and Committee on Committees

5. standing, joint, and special or select committees

6. legislative assistant, administrative assistant

7. closed, open, and modified rule

8. distributive policies and redistributive policies

True-False

1. The founding fathers viewed the House of Representatives as impulsive while the Senate was seen as more deliberative. T   F

2. By 1991 the percentage of African Americans in Congress finally came to equal the percentage of African Americans in the population as a whole. T   F

3. Logrolling is considered an unethical practice in Congress and may cost a member the election. T   F

4. Party whips in the House act as the heart of the party communication system. T   F

5. The most powerful individual in the Senate is the president pro tempore. T   F

6. A member who switches committees is able to transfer his seniority from the old committee to the new. T   F

7. Committee and subcommittee chairs are always held by the member from the majority party who holds the most seniority. T   F

8. Committee staffers are responsible for developing the legislation that comes from the committees. T   F

9. In the Committee of the Whole, the House can debate proposed laws under relaxed rules and with a smaller quorum. T   F

10. Once an effective and often used strategy, the filibuster has been rarely used since the Senate adopted Rule 22 on cloture. T   F

Multiple Choice

1. Each of the following is a specific power enumerated to Congress by the Constitution *except* the power to:
   a. levy taxes.
   b. pass bills of attainder.
   c. declare war.
   d. regulate commerce.

2. Most members of Congress see themselves as following the:
   a. trustee role.
   b. delegate role.
   c. politico role.
   d. party role.

3. Helping a constituent get information on a government program illustrates:
   a. casework.
   b. pork barrel politics.
   c. reciprocity.
   d. logrolling.

4. Legislative norms include:
   a. reciprocity.
   b. personal courtesy.
   c. subject specialization.
   d. all of the above

5. The Speaker of the House:
   a. is formally elected by the majority party caucus.
   b. is next in line to succeed the president after the vice-president.
   c. has essentially become a figure head position.
   d. acts as chairman of the Rules Committee.

6. The single most dominant individual in the Senate is the:
   a. majority whip.
   b. majority leader.
   c. president pro tempore.
   d. president of the Senate.

7. Compared with special or select committees, joint committees are:
   a. always larger in size.
   b. able to approve legislation.
   c. found only in the House.
   d. permanent rather than temporary.

8. Members of Congress are motivated to choose a particular committee in order to:
   a. enhance their reelection prospects.
   b. shape national policy.
   c. gain influence within Congress.
   d. all of the above

9. The agency that provides Congress with essential analysis of the economy and the economic impact of legislation is the:
   a. Congressional Research Service.
   b. Congressional Budget Office.
   c. Government Accountability Office.
   d. Office of Technology Assessment.

10. When a bill is "marked up" it means that the:
    a. bill's language and amendments have been decided upon.
    b. bill is being delayed by a filibuster.
    c. bill is being called up to bypass the Rules Committee.
    d. bill is bottled up in the Rules Committee.

11. Riders:
    a. must be germane to the legislation they are attached to.
    b. can only be used in the House of Representatives.
    c. are often used to force a president to accept a program he would otherwise veto.
    d. cannot be attached to general appropriations bills.

12. The Conference Committee:
    a. reconciles differences between the two parties in the House.
    b. has become primarily a formality.
    c. is often the scene of very hard bargaining and compromise.
    d. is closed to the public.

13. Lobbyists are most successful in affecting:
    a. distributive policies.
    b. redistributive policies.
    c. social welfare policies.
    d. economic policies.

14. Subgovernments or iron triangles:
    a. are most effective in influencing redistributive policy.
    b. work most effectively with media publicity.
    c. consist of congressional committees, bureaucratic agencies, and interest groups.
    d. all of the above

15. The President of the U.S. Senate is the:
    a. president.
    b. vice president.
    c. president pro tempore.
    d. majority leader.

Essay

1. What are the legislative norms that guide acceptable behavior in Congress? Comment on the problem of congressional ethics. Is the situation getting worse or better? Provide examples.

2. Compare and contrast the role of party leadership in the House with the role of party leadership in the Senate.

3. Explain and evaluate the committee system in Congress. Does it facilitate the legislative process or has it become cumbersome and unwieldy?

4. Do lobbyists help or hinder members of Congress in the performance of their jobs? Explain the reasons behind your opinion.

5. What do you believe will be the future role of a "changing Congress?" Give examples to support your answer.

Research Topics and Practical Applications

1. Investigate the representative from your home congressional district and write a short profile including the following information:
   a. personal characteristics (age, race, sex, education, former occupation, class status, etc.).
   b. political party and ideology.
   c. number of years in Congress.
   d. committee assignments and leadership positions in Congress.
   e. congressional roles (trustee, delegate, politico).
   f. frequency and record of voting on roll calls.
   g. legislation sponsored.
   h. media attention, such as extent of exposure.
   i. any other relevant information.

With this information at hand, evaluate your representative's performance in Congress.

2. Choose a recent bill that has passed Congress and trace its history through the legislative process. Try to determine when and where the bill originated, who introduced it, who supported it outside of Congress, which committees it went to, what changes were made (including amendments), how smoothly floor debate proceeded, who voted for it, and what happened after it passed Congress. How long did the whole process take and how was the bill changed from its original form?

ANSWER KEY

Completion

1. delegate
2. ombudsmen
3. Rules
4. seniority
5. Government Accountability Office
6. marked up
7. filibuster
8. iron triangles or subgovernments
9. Seventeenth Amendment
10. Casework

True-False

1. T
2. F
3. F
4. T
5. F
6. F
7. F
8. T
9. T
10. F

Multiple Choice

1. b
2. c
3. a
4. d
5. b
6. b
7. d
8. d
9. b
10. a
11. c
12. c
13. a
14. c
15. b

Chapter 10

THE PRESIDENCY

CHAPTER REVIEW

Learning Objectives

After studying Chapter 10 you should be able to:

1. Explain the fusion of symbolic and political authority in the American presidency.

2. Delineate the president's constitutional qualifications and powers.

3. Understand the role and importance of the organizations, agencies, and individuals who make up the executive branch.

4. Explain the relationship between the president and Congress over the direction and content of foreign and domestic policy.

5. Detail the particular skills the president needs to successfully guide his programs through Congress and lead his party.

6. Explain the relationship between the president and the media.

Chapter Outline and Summary

I.   Introduction

    A. Demands on the presidency are numerous and contradictory.

    B. Presidential influence and power has varied since the 1950s.

II. The President and Symbolic Leadership

    A. The president serves as both the ceremonial head of state and the actual head of government.

B. The ceremonial presidency is the symbol of national unity.

    1. The honeymoon period accords public goodwill and often results in political victories.

    2. International crises rally presidential support.

C. The fusion of symbolic and political authority may result in public criticism as well.

III. The President and the Constitution

  A. Introduction

    1. The Constitution requires the president to be a natural-born citizen, at least 35 years old, and a resident for 14 years.

    2. The president serves four-year terms, limited to two terms by the Twenty-second Amendment.

  B. Executive Power

    1. Presidents have interpreted executive power differently.

      a. The stewardship theory suggests broad powers.

      b. The constitutional theory suggests narrow, limited powers.

      c. The steel seizure case established a middle ground based on the imperatives of events.

    2. The plasticity of the presidency means that the president can mold the office according to his personality and events.

  C. The Power of Appointment

    1. The president nominates ambassadors, judges, and other officials, with the advice and consent of the Senate.

    2. The Senate may delay or defeat a nomination.

  D. The Removal Power

    1. The Supreme Court has ruled that the president's removal powers apply only to purely executive offices.

    2. The president can place pressure on officials to resign.

  E. The Power to Pardon

    1. The president's pardon powers are limited to federal offenses.

    2. Ford's pardon of Nixon was one of the most controversial.

IV. The President and the Executive Branch

    A. The Cabinet

        1. The Cabinet is not a high-level decision-making body.

        2. Individual officers can have significance for the president.

        3. Cabinet officers may be politically independent and more responsive to constituent groups than the president.

        4. The inner Cabinet consists of the secretaries of state, defense, homeland security, treasury, and the attorney general who work close to the president.

        5. The outer Cabinet consists of the remaining officers with defined programs and client groups.

        6. Recently presidents have chosen their cabinets based on loyalty and professionalism.

    B. The White House Staff

        1. Staff members are loyal to the president and usually close to the president prior to his assuming office.

        2. Staff aides offer advice, set legislative strategy, check the bureaucracy, review the Cabinet, plan the president's time, and say "no" for the president.

        3. Presidents manage their staff to suit their own personalities.

    C. The Executive Office of the President

        1. The Executive Office of the President (EOP) is the managerial arm of the presidency.

        2. The structure of the EOP reflects the dominant issues of the time and the office is used by presidents according to their own styles.

        3. The Office of Management and Budget helps the president develop the budget and monitors the president's programs.

        4. The National Security Council provides advice and policy coordination on questions of national security.

        5. The Council of Economic Advisers analyzes economic issues, makes economic forecasts, and prepares the president's Economic Report to Congress.

        6. The Office of Policy Development focuses on the formulation, coordination, and implementation of economic and domestic policy.

D. The Vice-President

    1. Most vice-presidents performed largely ceremonial tasks with the office a target of ridicule and disdain.

    2. More recently, vice-presidents have played a more important role as an advisor in policymaking.

E. Presidential Succession

    1. The Twenty-fifth Amendment allows the vice-president to become acting president when the president is disabled and provides a means to fill a vice-presidential vacancy.

    2. The Presidential Succession Act of 1947 establishes the line of succession in case of simultaneous vacancies.

V. The President and Congress: Foreign Policy

A. Introduction

    1. Congress can influence foreign policy, but the president controls it.

    2. Since Vietnam, Congress has become more assertive in foreign policy.

B. Negotiating Treaties

    1. Most treaties have been approved by the Senate without question (a major exception was the Treaty of Versailles).

    2. Since Wilson, presidents have included senators in treaty negotiations.

    3. Treaties are now rarely routine and often require presidential concessions.

C. Executive Agreements

    1. An executive agreement is an understanding between heads of state requiring no Senate approval.

    2. Many executive agreements have been serious tools of foreign policy, classified, and kept from Congress.

    3. The Case-Zablocki Act, primarily symbolic, placed restrictions on executive agreements, particularly secret ones.

VI. The President and Congress: The War Power

A. Introduction

    1. Congress alone has the constitutional power to declare war.

    2. The commander-in-chief clause establishes civilian control over the military.

B. The Mexican and Civil Wars

    1. James Polk manipulated Congress into declaring war on Mexico.

    2. Lincoln's actions before the Civil War were mostly backed by Congress and upheld by the Supreme Court in the Prize Cases.

C. The Two World Wars

    1. In 1917 and 1941 Congress formally declared war and delegated vast discretionary powers to the president.

    2. Roosevelt made broad use of his wartime powers, including the detention of all Japanese Americans (later upheld by the Court in *Korematsu v. United States*).

D. The Cold War

    1. Truman's action in the Korean War was outside the framers' original understanding of the president's war powers.

    2. During the Cold War, Congress acquiesced to the president's war powers, including Eisenhower's request to use force if needed to protect Taiwan.

E. The Vietnam Trauma

    1. Presidential war actions in Vietnam were sanctioned by Congress in the Gulf of Tonkin Resolution.

    2. As the war lost public support, Congress attempted to regain its authority primarily through its appropriations power.

F. The War Powers Resolution

    1. The War Powers Resolution states that the president cannot use troops in combat beyond 60 days unless authorized by Congress.

VII. The President and Congress: Domestic Policy

A. Legislative Skills—presidents must:

    1. know the legislative environment.

    2. have a good sense of timing.

    3. establish their priorities.

    4. have a high-quality legislative liaison office.

    5. consult with both party leaders.

    6. establish broad bipartisan support.

B. The Presidential Veto

    1. A president can veto a bill within ten days after which it can be overridden by a two-thirds majority of each house.

    2. A pocket veto, which cannot be overridden, occurs if Congress adjourns within the ten day period.

    3. The veto is a powerful weapon, few are overridden.

    4. The president does not have a line-item veto where only sections of a bill are rejected.

C. Executive Privilege

    1. Executive privilege is the right of the president to refuse information requested by Congress and the courts.

    2. Nixon attempted to enlarge this power during the Watergate affair, but the Court ruled in *United States v. Nixon* that executive privilege was not absolute.

    3. Congress has become more assertive and suspicious about claims of executive privilege (the Anne Burford/EPA case).

    4. President George W. Bush established the precedent for the National Security Advisor to testify in public under oath (for a non-criminal matter) for the 9/11 Commission.

D. Impeachment

    1. The House brings the impeachment charges and the Senate conducts the trial.

E. The Clinton Impeachment

    1. President Clinton became the second president to be impeached (charged with perjury and obstruction of justice) over the Monica Lewinsky affair.

VIII. The President and the Media

A. Introduction

    1. Presidents and the media have a love-hate relationship.

    2. Presidents want to control information while reporters want to get as much interesting information as possible.

    3. The media tend to oversimplify issues or treat personalities as stereotypes.

B. Phases of the Relationship

    1. Cooperation occurs in the administration's honeymoon stage.

    2. Conflict begins after the administration has settled in.

    3. Detachment occurs later as the president becomes less accessible to the press.

C. The Imperial President vs. the Imperial Media
1. The president can orchestrate his appearances, decide on the format, and use news leaks to his advantage.
2. The media can use investigative reporting, take advantage of news leaks, and portray the president as they wish.
3. The result is usually a stand-off between the president and the press.

IX. Summary

Key Terms, Concepts, and Personalities

After studying Chapter 10 you should be able to identify and describe the significance of:

Case-Zablocki Act

commander-in-chief clause

constitutional theory

Council of Economic Advisers (CEA)

executive agreements

Executive Office of the President

Gulf of Tonkin Resolution

head of government

head of state

impeachment

inner cabinet

line-item veto

multiple advocacy

National Security Council (NSC)

natural-born citizens

naturalized citizens

Office of Management and Budget (OMB)

Office of Policy Development (OPD)

outer cabinet

pocket veto

Presidential Succession Act of 1947

stewardship theory

the administration

Twenty-fifth Amendment

Twenty-second Amendment

veto

TESTING YOUR UNDERSTANDING

Completion

1. As head of state the president performs primarily _____ duties.

2. A third presidential term is forbidden by the _____ Amendment.

3. The broad interpretation of executive power often associated with Theodore Roosevelt is called the _____ _____.

4. The group of Cabinet members who handle issues of broad importance such as national security, economy, and justice is called the _____ _____.

5. George Bush's staged policy debates between his advisors is a process known as _____ _____.

6. Presidents can avoid the need for Senate ratification of treaties by entering into _____ _____ with foreign governments.

7. The Supreme Court ruled in the _____ Cases that Lincoln had acted in a proper constitutional fashion in his conduct of the Civil War.

8. The president does not possess a _____ veto, allowing him to veto sections of a bill.

9. The right of the president to refuse information requested by Congress and the courts is called _____ _____.

10. The third and last phase of the relationship between the president and the media is characterized by _____.

Compare and Contrast

1. head of state and head of government

2. natural-born citizens and naturalized citizens

3. stewardship theory and constitutional theory

4. inner Cabinet and outer Cabinet

5. Economic Policy Council and Domestic Policy Council

6. OMB, NSC, CEA, and OPD

7. Twenty-fifth Amendment and Presidential Succession Act of 1947

8. executive agreements and Case-Zablocki Act

9. line-item veto, pocket veto, and veto

10. executive privilege, Watergate affair, and *United States v. Nixon*

True-False

1. The Constitution requires the president to be a naturalized citizen, 35 years of age or older, and a resident of the United States for at least 14 years. T F

2. The Senate has the right to refuse a presidential appointment even if only on the grounds of opposition to a particular policy. T F

3. The Cabinet has historically been considered the president's closest policy advisors. T F

4. The primary responsibility of the Council of Economic Advisers is to help the president develop the annual federal budget. T F

5. The Case-Zablocki Act has for the most part made executive agreements a thing of the past. T F

6. During World War I Congress granted President Wilson almost dictatorial control over the economy. T F

7. The Gulf of Tonkin Resolution stipulates that before introducing troops into combat, the president must consult with Congress. T F

8. The president of the United States, unlike many governors, does not possess a line-item veto. T F

9. In *United States v. Nixon*, the Supreme Court declared that executive privilege is not an absolute right. T F

10. A president's endorsement of a candidate has little influence on voters. T F

Multiple Choice

1. According to the Constitution, a president must be:
   a. a natural born citizen.
   b. 35 years of age or older.
   c. a resident of the United States for at least 14 years.
   d. all of the above

2. Presidential pardon power:
   a. applies equally to federal and state and local laws.
   b. does not include clemency for a class of people.
   c. rarely gains headlines.
   d. may not be granted prior to a conviction or indictment.

3. Membership in the inner Cabinet does not include the:
   a. Secretary of Commerce.
   b. Secretary of the Treasury.
   c. Attorney General.
   d. Secretary of Defense.

4. Senior White House aides are responsible for:
   a. setting legislative strategy.
   b. keeping check on the bureaucracy.
   c. planning the president's time.
   d. all of the above

5. The executive office responsible for the formulation, coordination, and implementation of economic and domestic policy is the:
   a. Office of Management and Budget.
   b. National Security Council.
   c. Council of Economic Advisers.
   d. Office of Policy Development.

6. Treaties negotiated by the president of the United States:
   a. are rarely controversial and routinely ratified.
   b. require a two-thirds approval by the House of Representatives.
   c. often require presidential concessions.
   d. usually involve relatively minor matters.

7. The constitutional power to declare war belongs to the:
   a. courts.
   b. Congress.
   c. president.
   d. military.

8. Franklin Roosevelt:
   a. interned thousands of Japanese Americans in concentration camps.
   b. asserted wartime powers independent of Congress.
   c. transformed the nature of the presidency.
   d. all of the above

9. The Gulf of Tonkin Resolution:
   a. gave President Johnson broad authority to use military force in Southeast Asia.
   b. was passed unanimously in the House, but defeated in the Senate.
   c. was revoked by Congress only three months after being passed.
   d. requires the president to consult with Congress before introducing troops into combat.

10. The War Powers Resolution:
   a. has seriously limited the powers of the president.
   b. granted President Johnson extensive war powers during the Southeast Asian conflict.
   c. has had little effect on presidential behavior.
   d. was unanimously endorsed by both hawks and doves in the Senate.

11. An important presidential legislative skill is:
   a. a good sense of timing.
   b. a high quality legislative liaison office.
   c. consultation with leaders from both political parties.
   d. all of the above

12. A line-item veto:
   a. was opposed by President Reagan.
   b. is employed if Congress adjourns during the 10-day period after sending a bill to the president.
   c. is not available to the president.
   d. can be overridden by a two-thirds majority in each house.

13. Executive privilege:
   a. was upheld as constitutional in *United States v. Nixon*.
   b. is the right of the president to refuse information requested by Congress or the courts.
   c. has been rarely used in recent years.
   d. was granted to Reagan when Congress requested the testimony of EPA's Anne Burford.

14. The gap between what the public expects and what the president can do is greatest when it comes to:
   a. economic policy.
   b. foreign policy.
   c. environmental policy.
   d. military policy.

15. The only federal government officials to be convicted and removed from office were:
   a. senators.
   b. cabinet members.
   c. vice-presidents.
   d. judges.

16. During the honeymoon period of an administration the relationship between the president and the media can be characterized by:
   a. cooperation.
   b. conflict.
   c. detachment.
   d. hostility.

17. President Teddy Roosevelt believed in the _____ _____ concept of presidential authority.
   a. stewardship theory
   b. constitutional theory
   c. executive privilege
   d. executive agreement

18. The _____ is responsible for assembling the budget for the president.
   a. CEA
   b. NSC
   c. OPD
   d. OMB

19. The _____ provided for a mechanism for the vice-president to assume the presidency in the event of a presidential disability and the selection of a vice-president should that office become vacant.
   a. Nineteenth Amendment
   b. Twenty-second Amendment
   c. Twenty-fifth Amendment
   d. Twenty-sixth Amendment

20. When a president does not sign a piece of legislation within ten days and Congress has adjourned, it becomes a:
   a. law.
   b. veto.
   c. line-item veto.
   d. pocket veto.

Essay

1. What are the constitutional powers of the president? How have these powers been interpreted by different presidents? Give examples to illustrate your answer.

2. Who are the presidential advisors and aides? What roles do they play? Why are they so important to the president's ultimate success or failure? Give examples.

3. Using examples, describe how the president's war powers have changed since the nineteenth century. Explain the controversy between the president and Congress over war powers.

4. Why are some presidents more effective in getting their legislative proposals through Congress than others?

5. According to the text, presidents and the media are usually involved in a "love-hate relationship." Explain what is meant by this. What are the phases of the relationship between the president and the media?

Research Topics and Practical Applications

1. Presidents are often concerned about their historical reputations. Make a list of the factors that you believe might be used to rank a president as great, near great, above average, average, below average, or failure. Try placing the presidents in these various categories and then compare your rankings with those published by historians. Comment on whether greatness is thrust upon presidents by historical circumstances or whether a president can influence his own destiny.

2. Collect data from Gallup polls on presidential approval ratings since the Eisenhower Administration and comment on the following:
    a. How do the presidents compare in terms of their average approval rating and what factors might influence why some presidents are more popular than others?
    b. How has the approval rating fluctuated during each president's time in office? Is the honeymoon period apparent from the opinion data? Does the approval rating for each president generally increase or decline over time?
    c. Comment on how each president's changing approval rating might have been affected by the state of the economy, the international situation, and the individual president's relationship with the media during his time in office. Speculate about those influences that may have been especially important.

ANSWER KEY

Completion

1. ceremonial
2. Twenty-second
3. stewardship theory
4. inner Cabinet
5. multiple advocacy
6. executive agreements
7. Prize
8. line-item
9. executive privilege
10. detachment

True-False

1. F
2. T
3. F
4. F
5. F
6. T
7. F
8. T
9. T
10. T

Multiple Choice

1. d
2. c
3. a
4. d
5. d
6. c
7. b
8. d
9. a
10. c
11. d
12. c
13. b
14. a
15. d
16. a
17. a
18. d
19. c
20. d

Chapter 11

BUREAUCRACIES

CHAPTER REVIEW

After studying Chapter 11 you should be able to:

1. Define bureaucracy, delineate the main characteristics of bureaucracies, and explain who the bureaucrats are.

2. Describe the types of bureaucracies that compose the executive branch and explain their duties.

3. Discuss the origins of the contemporary civil service system.

4. Analyze the meaning of bureaucratic responsiveness and the relationship between the bureaucracy and the three branches of government.

5. Comment on the major criticisms of bureaucracies.

Chapter Outline and Summary

I. Bureaucracies As the Fourth Branch of Government

    A. Bureaucracies: Translating Ideas into Action

        1. Bureaucracies exist because translating ideas into actions requires an organization of people and resources for the task.

        2. A bureaucracy is a hierarchical organization that exists to accomplish public purposes (goals) characterized by expertise and impersonal rules.

    B. Who Are the Bureaucrats?

        1. Bureaucrat generally refers to any individual who works in the executive branch of government.

        2. Executive departments, independent establishments, and government corporations can almost be considered a fourth branch of government.

C. Distinguishing Characteristics of Bureaucracies

    1. Only bureaucracies are responsible for executing policies.

    2. Bureaucracies are extremely diverse.

    3. Bureaucracies are dispersed throughout Washington, D.C., but 86 percent of the bureaucrats work outside the capital.

    4 Most bureaucrats work in a relatively anonymous fashion.

    5. There is a wide range of jobs in the federal service.

II. Executive Branch Organization: Types of Bureaucracies

  A. The Executive Office of the President

    1. The president has a variety of staff advisers.

    2. Executive Office units allow the president to shape other bureaucracies.

  B. Executive Departments

    1. Department heads comprise the president's Cabinet.

    2. Cabinet changes reflect political judgments and pressures.

    3. Departments differ vastly in age, employees, and expenditures.

    4. Departments are really umbrellas for smaller bureaucratic units where the real work may be done (e.g., NIH).

  C. Independent Agencies

    1. Independent agencies are located outside executive departments.

    2. The determination of where to place an agency is strongly influenced by political considerations.

  D. Independent Regulatory Commissions

    1. Independent regulatory commissions are headed by a group of experts (commission) in a particular field.

    2. They lie outside executive departments, insulated from presidential control and partisan politics.

  E. Government Corporations

    1. Government corporations (e.g., U.S. Postal Service) offer a service for which the benefiting individual or institution must pay.

    2. They have a degree of financial and operational flexibility due to the commercial character of their work.

III. The Search for Competence in the Civil Service

    A. The Spoils System

        1. The spoils system is the practice of granting government jobs on the basis of party loyalty and election support.

        2. Ushered in by Andrew Jackson, the spoils system created the perception of corrupt government, with jobs bought and sold.

        3. Charles Guiteau's assassination of President Garfield triggered the public's call for reforms of the spoils system.

    B. The Pendleton Act and the Merit Principle

        1. The Pendleton Act (1883) established a Civil Service Commission to use merit as a condition of government employment.

        2. The Hatch Act (1939) banned civil servants from participation in partisan politics.

        3. The Office of Personnel Management employs exams, experience, and qualifications for employment.

        4. Clerical and administrative personnel are classified in a General Schedule (GS) based on experience and qualifications.

    C. The Civil Service Reform Act of 1978

        1. The Civil Service Reform Act of 1978 was intended to defend merit and provide incentives for high-quality work.

            a. A merit pay system was established for middle-level managers.

            b. Whistleblowers were protected from unfair retaliation.

            c. A Senior Executive Service (SES) was created with rewards and demotions built in based on performance.

            d. The Office of Personnel Management and Merit Systems Protection Board were created.

        2. The Act has suffered from lack of adequate funds and failure of the SES to become the prestigious group it was intended to be.

IV. The Search for Bureaucratic Responsiveness: The Political Environment of Bureaucracies

    A. The President

        1. The Constitution gives the president considerable authority over the bureaucracy.

        2. Presidential control over the bureaucracy is difficult.

            a. The large size of the bureaucracy makes close presidential supervision impossible.

            b. Bureaucrats are committed to their work, not the president.

3. Presidents do have resources to control the bureaucracy.

   a. Presidents can make some 3,000 bureaucratic appointments.

   b. Presidents can use the budget process to cut or increase financing of specific bureaucracies.

B. Congress

   1. Congress has several tools to control the bureaucracy.

      a. Congress can create and abolish agencies.

      b. The Senate must confirm presidential appointments.

      c. Congress can shape the amount and purpose of money spent by bureaucracies through its budget power.

      d. Congress can investigate bureaucratic behavior.

   2. Congressional members' reelection often depends on bureaucratic actions and performance.

C. The Case of the Legislative Veto

   1. The legislative veto, written into a law, could halt an executive initiative or agency action.

   2. The legislative veto was declared unconstitutional in *Immigration and Naturalization Service v. Chadha* (1983).

   3. The legislative veto continues, however, because of the need of Congress to control bureaucratic discretion.

D. Interest Groups

   1. Almost every bureaucratic unit has the strong support of some group and groups compete for influence over the agencies.

   2. Groups usually press claims on bureaucracies through such institutions as the mass media, courts, and Congress.

   3. Groups often have influence on public policy through iron triangles.

E. The Courts

   1. The courts can determine the constitutionality of congressional or presidential action, thus affecting bureaucracies.

   2. The courts attempt to ensure procedural fairness in the efforts of bureaucracies to promulgate rules and regulations.

   3. The courts discern the congressional intent behind vague legislation that has consequences for bureaucracies.

V. Bureaucrats and Government Regulation

   A. Regulation in Perspective

       1. The bureaucracy is responsible for considerable regulation activity.

       2. The continuing debate is whether the bureaucracy goes beyond congressional intent in their creation of rules.

   B. Regulatory Agencies and Types of Regulations

       1. There are economic and social regulations.

       2. Regulatory agencies perform both quasi-legislative and quasi-judicial functions.

   C. The Regulatory Process

       1. There is a complicated process followed for publishing regulations: slip law, *U.S. Statutes-at-Large*, *U.S. Code*, *Federal Register*, *Code of Federal Regulations*.

   D. The Ebb and Flow of Regulatory Debate

       1. Regulatory activity can be quite controversial since there are costs associated with any regulation.

           a. Cost-benefit analysis is used to determine the impact of proposed regulations.

VI. Bureaucracies: Targets and Mirrors of Conflict

   A. Introduction

       1. Bureaucracies are criticized for waste and fraud, although the government is always working to eliminate the problem.

       2. Bureaucracies are criticized for too much red tape, which is a problem for all groups in the political system and often is needed to provide safeguards.

       3. Bureaucracies are criticized for duplicating or conflicting with the work of other bureaucracies, but this may be explained by outside expectations.

       4. Bureaucracies are criticized for playing an independent political role, with three qualifications:

           a. In executing policy purposes, bureaucrats strive to achieve their institutions' goals.

           b. Bureaucrats have little discretion in translating ideas into action when laws are specific.

           c. Discretion is inevitable when laws are vague or ambiguous.

5. The issue of bureaucratic responsiveness centers on the determination of whose ideas ought to be translated into action.

VII. Summary

Key Terms, Concepts, and Personalities

After studying Chapter 11 you should be able to identify and describe the significance of:

bureaucracy
bureaucrat
Cabinet
Civil Service Reform Act of 1978
Code of Federal Regulations
deregulation
Federal Register
fourth branch
government corporation
Hatch Act
independent agency
independent regulatory commission
iron triangle
legislative veto

Merit Systems Protection Board
Office of Personnel Management (OPM)
Pendleton Act
public purpose
quasi-judicial
quasi-legislative
red tape
regulations
Senior Executive Service (SES)
slip law
spoils system
U.S. Code
U.S. Statutes-at-Large

TESTING YOUR UNDERSTANDING

Completion

1. The goals or objectives of a bureaucracy are called _____ _____.

2. The most distinguishing characteristic of bureaucracies is that only they are responsible for _____ public policies.

3. Civil servants contribute to the stability of governments by virtue of their capacity to meet political demands through their long _____ and _____.

4. One of the most important determinants of what purposes deserve Cabinet status is

   _____ _____.

5. The National Aeronautics and Space Administration and the Peace Corps are examples of _____ agencies.

6. The practice of making appointments to government jobs on the basis of party loyalty is called the _____ _____.

7. Clerical and administrative personnel within the competitive service are classified in a _____ _____ with 15 grades.

8. _____ has the ultimate responsibility for the creation and abolition of agencies.

9. To temper executive discretion and even halt an executive initiative, Congress created the

   _____ _____.

10. Often justified as a safeguard against abuse, bureaucracies have been criticized for wrapping their work in endless amounts of _____ _____.

Compare and Contrast

1. bureaucracy and public purpose

2. Max Weber, hierarchy, expertise, and rules

3. bureaucracy and fourth branch

4. Executive Office of the President and Cabinet

5. independent agency, independent regulatory commission, and government corporation

6. spoils system and Pendleton Act

7. Pendleton Act, Hatch Act, and Civil Service Reform Act of 1978

8. Senior Executive Service, Office of Personnel Management, and Merit Systems Protection Board

9. legislative veto and *Immigration and Naturalization Service v. Chadha*

True-False

1. In American government the term bureaucrat generally refers to any individual who works in the executive branch of government. T F

2. Almost ninety percent of all bureaucrats work outside of Washington, D.C. T F

3. Independent agencies are outside executive departments and their heads cannot be fired by the president. T F

4. Government corporations have remained loosely tied to the regular appropriations process much like other types of bureaucracies. T F

5. According to the Hatch Act, civil servants are banned from participation in partisan political activity. T F

6. The Senior Executive Service has become a highly prestigious and respected group of senior civil servants, much like those in Great Britain. T F

7. Salaries for public officials are usually equal or above the compensation rates for equivalent positions in the private sector. T F

8. Nearly every bureaucratic unit has the strong support of some interest group. T F

9. When laws are vague or ambiguous, bureaucratic discretion is inevitable. T F

10. The *U.S. Code* is a chronological compilation, by year, of slip laws passed in each session of Congress. T F

Multiple Choice

1. Since the nation's founding, the most explosive growth in government has occurred in the:
   a. Congress and its staff.
   b. presidency and the president's personal staff.
   c. development and evolution of bureaucracies.
   d. number of courts and judges.

2. According to Max Weber, an ideal bureaucracy consists of:
   a. expertise.
   b. impersonal rules.
   c. a hierarchical division of labor.
   d. all of the above

3. Most federal bureaucrats:
   a. live and work in the Washington D.C. area.
   b. are involved in the execution of public policies.
   c. receive enormous media attention.
   d. are employed as clerks and office workers.

4. The president's cabinet is composed of:
   a. the heads of the units in the Executive Office of the President.
   b. the heads of the executive departments.
   c. the president's personal and closest advisors.
   d. all of the above

5. The executive department with the largest budget is the:
   a. Department of Defense.
   b. Department of State.
   c. Department of Treasury.
   d. Department of Health and Human Services.

6. Independent agencies are called independent because:
   a. they are outside the regular appropriations process.
   b. the president cannot hire or fire their heads.
   c. they are located outside of the executive departments.
   d. they are not influenced by interest groups.

7. Independent regulatory commissioners:
    a. were intended to be experts, insulated from partisan politics.
    b. have fixed terms, often longer than the president's.
    c. can be removed only for causes specified in statutory law.
    d. all of the above

8. An example of a government corporation is the:
    a. Federal Deposit Insurance Corporation.
    b. Interstate Commerce Commission.
    c. Small Business Administration.
    d. all of the above

9. Government employment during the administration of George Washington was characterized by:
    a. corruption.   c. integrity and honor.
    b. political spoils.   d. lack of respect and prestige.

10. Merit as a condition of government employment was established by the:
    a. Pendleton Act.
    b. Hatch Act.
    c. Civil Service Reform Act.
    d. Merit Systems Protection Act.

11. The Hatch Act:
    a. established merit as a condition of government employment.
    b. banned civil servants from participation in partisan politics.
    c. provided incentives for high-quality work by civil servants.
    d. established the Senior Executive Service.

12. The Civil Service Reform Act of 1978:
    a. has gone beyond expectations in establishing a prestigious and respected civil service.
    b. banned civil servants from participation in partisan politics.
    c. created a General Schedule to classify civil servants according to 15 grades based on experience and qualifications.
    d. provided protections for individuals who report waste or fraud in the bureaucracy.

13. One of the tools the president has to make bureaucrats more responsive is the power to:
    a. propose cuts or increases in the budgets of bureaucracies.
    b. create or abolish agencies.
    c. investigate bureaucratic power.
    d. all of the above

14. Each of the following is a means by which Congress can shape bureaucratic behavior except:
    a. create or abolish agencies.
    b. shape the amount and purpose of money bureaucrats spend.
    c. appoint high level administrators to departments and agencies.
    d. investigate bureaucratic behavior.

15. The legislative veto:
    a. allows the president to invalidate congressional laws affecting the bureaucracy.
    b. continues to be written into some statutes.
    c. was upheld in *Immigration and Naturalization Service v. Chadha.*
    d. is used to delegate discretionary authority to the president.

16. Interest groups:
    a. sometimes have a proprietary interest in specific agencies.
    b. may compete as they press their claims on the same bureaucratic unit.
    c. utilize the media, courts, and Congress to press claims on bureaucracies.
    d. all of the above

17. The group with the most passive role in controlling the political environment of bureaucracies is:
    a. the courts.   c. interest groups.
    b. Congress.   d. the presidency.

18. The most common way courts affect bureaucracies is when they:
    a. discern the congressional intent behind vague or ambiguous legislation.
    b. ensure procedural fairness in bureaucracies.
    c. declare congressional and presidential actions unconstitutional.
    d. create or abolish bureaucratic agencies.

19. The most serious criticism of bureaucrats is that they:
    a. waste and defraud public resources.
    b. affect public policies and play an unintended political role.
    c. wrap their work in unnecessary amounts of red tape.
    d. do work that duplicates or conflicts with other bureaucrat's work.

20. The daily governmental publication that contains proposed and final regulations, presidential proclamations, and executive orders.
    a. slip laws
    b. *U.S. Statutes-at-Large*
    c. *U.S. Code*
    d. *Federal Register*

Essay

1. Who are the bureaucrats and what are the distinguishing characteristics of bureaucracies?

2. Summarize the history of reform of the civil service. Why is it difficult to reform the civil service system?

3. Review the various institutions, organizations, or individuals that can control bureaucratic behavior. Which do you feel is the most effective and why?

4. What are the major criticisms of bureaucracies and how might these criticisms be answered?

Research Topics and Practical Applications

1. Consult the most recent *U.S. Government Manual* for information on government agencies. Choose an agency that might be of interest to you and write a profile of this agency. Include in your profile information or insight on the following:
    a. date of origin.
    b. type of agency.
    c. head of the agency.
    d. number of employees.
    e. size of the agency budget.
    f. function or purpose of the agency.
    g. interest group involvement in the agency.

h. any recent controversies or media attention.

i. political influence of the agency.

What does your profile of this agency tell you about bureaucracies and bureaucrats in general?

2. This chapter examines the federal bureaucracies. State governments also need an extensive bureaucracy to perform the daily functions of the state. Examine the bureaucracy in your home state or the state in which your college or university is located. Find or make an organizational chart for your state government similar to the one found in Figure 11.1 in your text. How does the organization of the state differ from the organization of the federal government and how is it the same? Which departments and agencies are similar and which are different? What are the departments or agencies that exist in one government but not the other? What does this tell you about the different functions of the state and federal governments?

ANSWER KEY

Completion

1. public purposes
2. implementing
3. tenure, expertise
4. political support
5. independent
6. spoils system
7. General Schedule
8. Congress
9. legislative veto
10. red tape

True-False

1. T
2. T
3. F
4. F
5. T
6. F
7. F
8. T
9. T
10. F

Multiple Choice

1. c
2. d
3. b
4. b
5. d
6. c
7. d
8. a
9. c
10. a
11. b
12. d
13. a
14. c
15. b
16. d
17. a
18. a
19. b
20. d

Chapter 12

THE SUPREME COURT AND THE
AMERICAN JUDICIARY

CHAPTER REVIEW

Learning Objectives

After studying Chapter 12 you should be able to:

1. Describe the structure of the federal, state, and local court systems, comparing them in terms of jurisdiction and types of cases heard.

2. Explain the criteria used for selecting federal judges.

3. Understand the various functions performed by American courts.

4. Discuss the working dynamics of the Supreme Court of the United States, particularly how cases are decided through five distinct stages.

5. List and explain the factors that influence decision-making in the Supreme Court as well as the checks on judicial power.

Chapter Outline and Summary

I. The National Court System

    A. Introduction

        1. There are three distinguishing factors about the courts.

            a. The judiciary operates only in the context of cases.

            b. Cases develop in a strictly prescribed fashion.

            c. Judges rely heavily on reason in justifying what they do.

        2. Cases: Raw Material for the Judiciary

            a. A case refers to a dispute handled by a court.

            b. Criminal cases involve a crime or public wrong against society.

            c. Civil cases are actions involving a private wrong or dispute.

B. Fifty-one Judicial Systems

   1. The national court system consists of state courts and federal courts, each hearing different kinds of cases.

   2. Jurisdiction refers to the authority a court has to hear a case in terms of the parties and subject matter involved.

   3. State and federal courts are both bound by the Constitution and each may have cases appealed to the U.S. Supreme Court.

C. State and Local Courts

   1. These courts handle the great bulk of legal business.

   2. State judicial systems are usually divided into four tiers.

     a. Courts of limited jurisdiction hear minor cases in villages, towns, and cities usually decided by a judge alone.

     b. Courts of general jurisdiction usually located in each county hear appeals and serious criminal offenses and civil suits.

     c. Intermediate appellate courts accept appeals from courts of general jurisdiction.

     d. Courts of last resort (usually state supreme courts) hear final appeals.

   3. Most state judges are elected. In some instances the Missouri Plan allows the governor to appoint judges from a list of nominees.

   4. Judges may be subject to periodic retention votes.

D. United States District Courts

   1. The Judiciary Act of 1789 organized a national court system.

   2. The 94 United States district courts hear almost all federal cases and some state cases through diversity jurisdiction.

E. United States Courts of Appeals

   1. There are 13 United States courts of appeals with 12 having a regional jurisdiction or circuit.

   2. Appeals judges sit in panels of three and hear cases on appeal from district courts or the tax court and review rulings from federal agencies.

   3. The Court of Appeals for the Federal Circuit hears appeals in patent cases as well as all appeals from the Claims court, Court of International Trade, and Court of Veterans Appeals.

F. Special Courts

1. Tribunals created by Congress to hear specific kinds of cases include Claims Court, Court of International Trade, Tax Court, Court of Veterans Appeals, and Court of Military Appeals.

2. Except for the Court of International Trade, these are legislative courts created by Congress to assist with implementation of statutes.

3. Judges in constitutional courts are appointed by the president and serve during good behavior, while Congress specifies the appointment and terms of judges in legislative courts.

G. The Supreme Court of the United States

1. The Court has appellate jurisdiction from cases in federal courts and the highest state courts when federal questions are raised.

2. Almost all cases reach the Court on a writ of certiorari and at least four justices must agree to accept a case (rule of four).

3. The Court has original jurisdiction in four kinds of disputes.

    a. Cases between one of the states and the U.S. government.

    b. Cases between two or more states.

    c. Cases involving foreign ambassadors, ministers, or consuls.

    d. Cases begun by a state against a citizen of another state or country. (The Eleventh Amendment requires suits against a state by a citizen of another state or country to go to the state court.)

    e. Today only cases between states qualify exclusively as original cases for the Supreme Court.

4. The Court is headed by the chief justice of the United States whose vote counts the same as the other eight associate justices.

H. Federal Judicial Selection

1. All federal judges are appointed by the president and confirmed by the Senate.

2. Federal judges have no constitutional qualifications.

3. Senatorial courtesy allows home-state senators to strongly influence the fate of presidential nominees.

4. The American Bar Association rates the qualification of nominees.

5. A president's selection of a Supreme Court justice is based upon professional qualifications, Senate acceptability, ideological fit, personal friendship, and background factors.

6. Supreme Court justices have not been generally representative of American society.

7. Senate confirmation is not automatic; several recent nominees have been rejected.

I. The Clarence Thomas Affair

1. Democrats opposed Thomas' nomination since he was conservative and they believed he would threaten civil liberties and civil rights.

2. Allegations of sexual harassment further politicized his nomination.

3. He was eventually confirmed by a slim margin.

II. What Courts Do

A. Cases: Raw Material for the Judiciary
1. A criminal case tries someone for an alleged crime.

2. A civil case is non-criminal such as a divorce, child custody and personal injury.

B. Constitutional Interpretation

1. Judicial review allows a court to set aside laws made by elected officials if judges believe the law violates the Constitution.

2. Groups that have failed in the executive or legislative branches often resort to the courts.

C. Statutory Interpretation

1. Often courts are required to interpret laws that may be vague.

2. Judges may need to discover legislative intent when unanticipated situations arise affecting a bill, such as the case of the use of videotape and copyright laws.

D. Fact Determination

1. Judges select from competing testimony and evidence that they believe to be true and false.

2. Fact determination is most visible in a trial court.

E. Clarification of the Boundaries of Political Authority

1. Courts attempt to resolve conflicts between the branches of government over the exercise of power.

2. In 1952 the Supreme Court declared President Truman had exceeded his powers by seizing the steel mills.

F. Education and Value Application

  1. Judges teach and apply values when making decisions.

  2. Through opinion leaders, court decisions help shape public attitudes.

G. Legitimization

  1. In most cases, courts provide legitimacy by upholding challenged laws or policies.

  2. The Supreme Court's decision to uphold the civil rights laws of the 1960s virtually ended the controversy.

III. The Supreme Court at Work

  A. Petition for Review

    1. Lawyers file briefs with the Court's clerk, requesting that the Court consider the issues raised in the case.

    2. Cases are either decided with full opinion, decided summarily, without opinion, or denied review.

    3. Chances for review are enhanced if one or more factors exist.

      a. The United States is a party to the case.

      b. Different courts of appeals have decided differently.

      c. The case involves an issue the justices want to resolve.

      d. A lower court has made a decision at odds with the established Supreme Court interpretations.

      e. The Court's workload permits acceptance of another case.

      f. The case represents a critical national issue.

  B. Briefs on the Merits

    1. A second round of briefs focus on the decision the justices should make.

    2. *Amicus curiae* briefs are submitted by "friends of the court" with an interest in the case.

    3. The solicitor general of the United States represents the government before the Supreme Court.

  C. Oral Argument

    1. Each side is given 30 minutes for oral argument with justices asking questions as desired.

    2. Appearance before the Court is an intimidating experience.

D. Conference and Decision

    1. After oral arguments, the justices meet to discuss the case.

    2. If opinions are unclear, a non binding vote is taken.

    3. Conferences are closed and leaks are rare.

E. Assignment and Writing of Opinions

    1. An opinion of the Court is a consensus explanation and justification of the decision agreed to by at least a bare majority of the justices.

    2. Dissenting opinions are written by justices in the minority.

    3. Concurring opinions are written by majority justices whose reasons differ or who have other thoughts to add.

    4. All opinions are published in the *United States Reports*.

F. Law Clerks

    1. Law clerks (recent law school graduates) assist the justices.

    2. Clerks do a variety of jobs and work long hours.

IV. The Supreme Court and American Government: An Assessment

A. Judicial Review and Democracy

    1. Critics argue that judicial review is antidemocratic, for judges invalidate decisions made by elected representatives.

    2. Others reply that judicial review checks government power and protects minority rights.

B. Influences on Supreme Court Decision Making

    1. Justice's own political ideas have a strong influence.

    2. A justice's perception of his/her role is a strong influence.

        a. Some justices are result-oriented, seeing their task as writing political ideas into their decisions.

        b. Some justice's are process-oriented, concerned with the Court's place in the democratic process.

        c. Judicial activists are eager to apply judicial review, judicial restraintists are not.

    3. Precedents, prior decisions in similar cases, affect justices' decisions.

    4. The Court's own decision-making process (briefs and oral arguments) shape its decisions.

    5. Collegial interaction and conferences affect decisions.

    6. Public opinion may influence the actions of the justices.

C. Checks on Judicial Power

    1. Constitutional amendments may reverse a Court's decision.

    2. Statutory amendment allows Congress to correct the Court's interpretation of a statute.

    3. Impeachment may be used to remove judges and justices.

    4. Congress may withdraw jurisdiction from the lower federal courts or change their size.

    5. The president may appoint and Senate confirm new justices.

    6. The Court depends on others for compliance, sometimes requiring litigation.

V. Summary

Key Terms, Concepts, and Personalities

After studying Chapter 12 you should be able to identify and describe the significance of:

amicus curiae

appellate jurisdiction

brief

civil case

concurring opinion

court of last resort

courts of general jurisdiction

courts of limited jurisdiction

criminal case

dissenting opinion

dual court system

Eleventh Amendment

federal courts

federal question

intermediate appellate courts

judicial activists

judicial restraintists

judicial review

jurisdiction

Missouri Plan

opinion of the Court

oral argument

original jurisdiction

precedents

rule of four

senatorial courtesy

Solicitor General of the United States

stare decisis

state courts

United States courts of appeals

United States district courts

TESTING YOUR UNDERSTANDING

Completion

1. Almost all divorce and personal injury cases are heard in _____ courts.

2. Questions of state law may get into district court through _____ _____.

3. The _____ Court hears suits involving monetary damages against the United States government.

4. Today, almost all cases reach the Supreme Court on a writ of _____.

5. The practice that allows home-state senators considerable control over the fate of presidential judicial nominees is called _____ _____.

6. Petitions for review filed by lawyers with the Supreme Court's clerk are called _____.

7. Prior decisions in similar court cases are called _____.

8. Congress and the states may correct the Supreme Court's interpretation of the Constitution through a _____ _____.

9. The concept of _____ _____ allows the judiciary to declare an executive action or legislative act as unconstitutional and therefore, null and void.

10. The judiciary is discussed in _____ of the Constitution.

Compare and Contrast

1. criminal cases and civil cases

2. state courts and federal courts

3. courts of limited jurisdiction, courts of general jurisdiction, intermediate appellate courts, and court of last resort

4. appellate jurisdiction and original jurisdiction

5. judicial review and legislative intent

6. majority opinion, dissenting opinion, and concurring opinion

7. judicial activists and judicial restraintists

True-False

1. The judiciary operates only in the context of cases. T F

2. The United States Supreme Court can decide only cases that originate in federal courts. T F

3. Most state judges are appointed for life and can be removed only by impeachment. T F

4. Presidents overwhelmingly appoint members of their own political party to the federal bench. T F

5. About half the cases the Supreme Court decides involve the meaning the justices give to words legislators have written. T F

6. The Supreme Court usually writes a decision for the majority of the cases on its docket each term. T F

7. Supreme Court conferences and deliberations are open to the public. T F

8. The written opinion of the Supreme Court represents a consensus of the majority of justices. T F

9. The most often used check on judicial power has been impeachment. T F

10. The constitutional authority for the judiciary can be found in Article IV, Section 3, of the Constitution. T F

Multiple Choice

1. An attempt to recover damages following an automobile accident would be considered a:
   a. criminal case.
   b. civil case.
   c. federal case.
   d. appellate case.

2. State courts that serve as trial courts for serious criminal offenses are:
   a. courts of limited jurisdiction.
   b. courts of general jurisdiction.
   c. intermediate appellate courts.
   d. courts of last resort.

3. The Missouri Plan:
   a. allows state governors to appoint judges from a list of nominees.
   b. requires judges to be elected for five-year terms.
   c. is a recall device used to remove undesirable state judges.
   d. requires judges to run as independents without party affiliation.

4. Almost all federal cases begin in the:
   a. courts of general jurisdiction.
   b. United States courts of appeal.
   c. United States district courts.
   d. state courts.

5. Each of the following is a legislative court except the:
   a. Tax Court.
   b. Claims Court.
   c. Court of Military Appeals.
   d. Court of International Trade.

6. The Supreme Court's original jurisdiction includes cases:
   a. between one of the states and the United States government.
   b. between two or more states.
   c. involving foreign ambassadors, ministers, or consuls.
   d. all of the above

7. Dwight Eisenhower's choice of Earl Warren as Chief Justice of the Supreme Court:
   a. proved to be a very popular choice.
   b. resulted in a series of judicial reforms.
   c. resulted in landmark cases involving social reform.
   d. moved the Court in a conservative direction.

8. Throughout history, most Supreme Court justices have:
   a. been active in public affairs or have held political office.
   b. come from ethnic or minority backgrounds.
   c. come form a variety of religious backgrounds.
   d. been representative of American society.

9. The process by which judges attempt to figure out the meaning of particular laws passed by Congress or state legislatures is called:
   a. judicial review.
   b. legislative intent.
   c. fact determination.
   d. legitimization.

10. Fact determination is most visible in:
    a. the Supreme Court.
    b. legislative courts.
    c. trial courts.
    d. intermediate appellate courts.

11. Chances for review by the Supreme Court are significantly increased if the:
    a. United States is a party to the case and requests review.
    b. case involves an issue some of the justices are eager to resolve.
    c. Court's work load permits accepting another case for decision.
    d. all of the above

12. Documents submitted to the Court from interest groups and others who are not parties to the case but have a stake in its outcome are called:
    a. *amicus curiae* briefs.
    b. writs of *certiorari*.
    c. arraignments.
    d. dissenting opinions.

13. The United States government's lawyer before the Supreme Court is called the:
    a. special prosecutor.
    b. solicitor general.
    c. federal district attorney.
    d. chief justice.

14. Oral arguments before the Supreme Court:
    a. are held in private.
    b. may last for hours.
    c. give the justices a chance to ask questions about the case.
    d. have virtually no influence on the outcome of a case.

15. Franklin Roosevelt's court-packing plan:
    a. increased the size of the Supreme Court bench to 15.
    b. resulted in a more conservative Supreme Court.
    c. was a ploy to create seats for new justices who would support the president's programs.
    d. became law in 1937.

16. Supreme Court decision-making is influenced by:
    a. the justice's own political ideas.
    b. public opinion.
    c. collegial interaction.
    d. all of the above

17. A judicial restraintist:
    a. is eager to apply judicial review.
    b. finds constitutional standards hard to meet.
    c. is wary of going against the wishes of elected representatives.
    d. often changes the decisions made by other branches of government.

18. Checks on judicial power include:
    a. constitutional amendment.
    b. impeachment.
    c. withdrawing jurisdiction.
    d. all of the above

19. The existence of the lower federal courts (i.e., district courts and appellate courts) is up to:
    a. the Supreme Court.
    b. the president.
    c. Congress.
    d. the bureaucracy.

20. Courts do the following:
    a. constitutional interpretation.
    b. statutory interpretation.
    c. legitimization.
    d. all of the above

Essay

1. Diagram the federal and state court systems in the United States, noting the jurisdiction and functions of the courts at each level of your diagram.

2. Explain the process by which federal judges are selected, particularly Supreme Court justices. What factors do presidents consider when choosing a nominee? Why might the Senate turn down a presidential nominee? Give examples.

3. Discuss the functions that the courts perform for American politics and society.

4. What are the factors that influence how the Supreme Court justices make their decisions? Which factors do you believe are the most important and why?

5. Review the various checks on judicial power. Which would seem more politically effective and why? Give examples.

Research Topics and Practical Applications

1. In the summer of 1991 President George Bush nominated Judge Clarence Thomas of the U.S. Court of Appeals for the District of Columbia Circuit to replace Justice Thurgood Marshall on the Supreme Court. Present an analysis of this decision. Write a brief biographical sketch of Clarence Thomas including such relevant factors such as home state, race, religion, gender, education, former employment, party affiliation, ideology, political activities, and any other factors you might deem relevant. What factors do you believe most influenced President Bush's decision and why? What groups supported and opposed the nomination and why? Summarize the Senate confirmation process including the judiciary committee hearings and floor debate. You could use reports from the popular news media and/or government publications as information sources.

2. One of the best ways to gain an understanding of the American judicial system is to observe it in action. Visit your local county court house and sit in on a trial in process. Take notes of what you observe. Pay particular attention to the type of cases, the number of cases, how the lawyers present their cases, how decisions are made, what decisions are made, and the process as a whole. If possible you may wish to briefly interview someone associated with the process, whether it be a judge, lawyer, bailiff, or clerk to get their insights. Afterward, write a critical analysis of what you learned, commenting on the fairness of the American judicial system.

ANSWER KEY

Completion

1. state
2. diversity jurisdiction
3. Claims
4. certiorari
5. senatorial courtesy
6. briefs
7. precedents
8. constitutional amendment
9. judicial review
10. Article III

True-False

1. T
2. F
3. F
4. T
5. T
6. F
7. F
8. T
9. F
10. F

Multiple Choice

1. b
2. b
3. a
4. c
5. d
6. d
7. c
8. a
9. b
10. c
11. d
12. a
13. b
14. c
15. c
16. d
17. c
18. d
19. c
20. d

Chapter 13

GOVERNMENT AND PUBLIC POLICY

CHAPTER REVIEW

Learning Objectives

After studying Chapter 13 you should be able to:

1. Define public policy.

2. Describe various models of policymaking.

3. Discuss contrasting theories of who makes policy decisions.

4. Describe the two approaches to policymaking, the rational-comprehensive approach and incrementalism.

5. Delineate the stages in the policy process and discuss the roles played by the relevant actors in each stage.

6. Understand the role of economic self-interest in politics.

7. Itemize and explain the various categories of national government policies.

Chapter Outline and Summary

I. Public Policy in the Political Process

  A. Conflict over the Ends of Government

    1. Public policy is "whatever governments choose to do or not to do."
    2. Debates over procedures and rules are really debates over policy.
    3. Policy results mirror conflicts in demands resulting in varying consequences for different groups.
    4. Even policies designed to protect the common good may have differential consequences.

B. Perspectives on Policymaking

    1. Several models or explanations of policymaking have been proposed.

        a. The systems model holds that policy is the product of an interlocking relationship between institutions of government and its social, economic, and political environment.

        b. The bureaucratic model holds that bureaucracies play a crucial role in making policy because of their commitment and the expertise they can provide.

        c. The Marxism model holds that public policy decisions in non-Marxist regimes reflect the interests of the ruling economic class at the expense of the workers.

        d. The free market capitalism model holds that government plays a limited role and the natural forces of supply and demand are thus allowed to prevail in the marketplace.

    2. *Who* makes policy decisions?

        a. According to the elitism model, public policy decisions are made by a relatively small group of individuals acting in their own self-interest rather than in the interest of the mass of citizens.

        b. According to the pluralism model, public policy decisions are the result of struggle among contesting groups that reflect the various interest among citizens.

    3. *How* are policy decisions made?

        a. In the rational-comprehensive model, policymakers identify problems, consider various policy alternatives and their costs and benefits, and select and implement the policy strategy with the highest benefits and the lowest costs.

        b. Incrementalism is an alternative model that holds that new policies should differ only marginally from existing policies.

C. Stages in the Policy Process

    1. The policy process is a confusing clash of ideas, events, and personalities.

    2. Five stages in the evolution of policies help make sense out of a seemingly confusing and chaotic process. (See Figure 13.1)

    3. Getting Issues on the Agenda of Government

        a. The policy agenda is comprised of the list of issues that engage the attention of elected officials.

        b. The issues on the policy agenda are always changing.

        c. Different sets of issues have dominated the policy agenda at different times.

    4. Formulating Policy Proposals

        a. In this stage debate centers around policy strategy, the course of action designed to deal with the original problem.

b. What government should do, who should benefit, and who should bear the costs comprise the material of policy debate.

    5. Adopting Policy Proposals

        a. Policy adoption occurs when the institutions of government make a formal, authoritative decision.

        b. Formal adoption may occur through the passage of a bill, a Supreme Court decision, or a bureaucratic regulation.

    6. Implementing Policies—Bureaucracies are ultimately responsible for policy implementation, translating policy ideas into action.

    7. Evaluating Policies—Policy evaluation determines whether the formally adopted, implemented strategy did ameliorate the originally defined problem.

II. The Actors

  A. Introduction

    1. The president, Congress, bureaucracy, judiciary, interest groups, and the media are major actors in the policy process.

  B. The states and political parties also influence policy making.

III. The Purposes and Presence of the National Government

  A. Introduction

    1. Two basic policy categories are domestic policy and foreign policy.

  B. Politics and Economic Self-Interest

    1. The presence or absence of economic self-interest is another useful criterion for differentiating policies.

  C. Categories of National Government Policies

    1. *Foreign and defense policies* are among the oldest functions of the national government.

    2. *Social welfare* activities represent the most significant growth in the role of government over the past half-century.

    3. *Protection of legal and constitutional rights* is exemplified by Supreme Court decisions protecting individual and group rights and congressional legislation on civil and voting rights.

    4. *Promotion of science and technology* has become government policy in such areas as the space program and medical research.

5. *Regulation* by government is intended to structure relationships in certain industries or enhance the political and economic status of certain groups.

6. *Economic policies* have their roots in the early days of the Republic and continue to have a huge impact through budget, tax, employment, investment, and other policies.

IV. Summary

Key Terms, Concepts, and Personalities

After studying Chapter 13 you should be able to identify and describe the significance of:

bureaucratic model	policy adoption
domestic policy	policy agenda
elitism	policy evaluation
foreign policy	policy implementation
free market capitalism model	policy strategy
incrementalism	public policy
Marxism model	rational-comprehensive model
pluralism	systems model

TESTING YOUR UNDERSTANDING

Completion

1. Debates over procedures and rules are really debates over _____.

2. The list of issues that engage the attention of elected officials is called the _____ _____.

3. A specific course of action designed to deal with the originally defined problem is called a policy _____.

4. The _____ model of policymaking holds that policy is the product of an interlocking relationship between institutions of government and its surrounding social, economic, and political environment.

5. _____ holds that a small group of individuals actually formulate policy.

6. One approach to policymaking is that of _____, in which policy decisions vary only marginally from previous policy.

7. The translation of policy ideas into action is called _____ _____.

8. The goal of _____ _____ is to determine whether the formally adopted, implemented strategy did in fact solve the original problem.

9. The _____ _____ of policy making holds that bureaucracies play a crucial role in making policy because of their commitment and the expertise they can provide.

10. _____ asserts that public policy decisions are the result of the struggle among contesting groups rather than a single elite.

Compare and Contrast

1. policy agenda, strategy, adoption, implementation, and evaluation

2. systems model, bureaucratic model, Marxism model, free market capitalism model

3. elitism, pluralism

4. rational-comprehensive model, incrementalism

5. bureaucracies and policy implementation

True-False

1. Policies that are designed to protect some common good always affect everyone in the same way. T F

2. The political will of a strong leader may help move some particular issue onto the government agenda. T F

3. An example of formal policy adoption may be a decision by the Supreme Court.   T   F

4. When a policy is formally and legally implemented, debate over the issue usually ends.   T   F

5. Economic self-interest plays little or no role in policymaking.   T   F

6. It is required by law that every government policy must go through a formal evaluation procedure.   T   F

7. The judiciary establishes policy with their court rulings.   T   F

Multiple Choice

1. Public policymaking:
   a. is nonconflictual in a democratic system.
   b. involves debate over rules but not procedures.
   c. has varying consequences for different groups.
   d. is designed to protect the common good.

2. The decision to deal with the drug abuse problem by opening more treatment centers would be an example of a:
   a. policy agenda.
   b. policy strategy.
   c. policy adoption.
   d. policy implementation.

3. Which of the following statements about policy adoption is true?
   a. Supreme Court decisions are not a form of policy adoption.
   b. The adoption of a particular course of action resolves most conflicts among proponents and opponents.
   c. The failure to adopt a policy proposal is a form of policymaking.
   d. Regulatory agencies are not involved in policy adoption, only in implementation.

4. The idea that policy decisions reflect the interest of the ruling class at the expense of the workers is a tenet of the:
   a. elitism model.
   b. pluralism model.
   c. Marxism model.
   d. free market capitalism model.

5. Incrementalism is an approach to policy whereby:
   a. the costs and benefits of a proposed policy are weighed.
   b. policymaking is based on the economic self-interest of the group making the decision.
   c. new policy should vary only marginally from previous policy.
   d. bureaucracies act in a critical role in policymaking due to their commitment and expertise.

6. Bureaucracies play a central role in the policy process during the:
   a. agenda building stage.
   b. policy proposal stage.
   c. policy adoption stage.
   d. implementation stage.

7. The final analytical stage in the evolution of policies is:
   a. evaluation.
   b. agenda-building.
   c. implementation.
   d. adoption.

8. Policy evaluation:
   a. is required by law.
   b. formally ends the policy debate.
   c. usually occurs informally during the implementation process.
   d. has become increasingly accurate with precise measures.

9. The _____ sets the tone for policy making.
   a. president
   b. judiciary
   c. Congress
   d. bureaucracy

10. The _____ is responsible for implementing policy.
    a. president
    b. judiciary
    c. Congress
    d. bureaucracy

Essay

1. Explain what is meant by "public policy results mirror conflicts in demands." Use examples to illustrate your explanation.

2. How is the policy agenda formulated? What factors influence what issues might be placed on the agenda and how has the policy agenda changed over time?

3. How are public policies evaluated? Why is policy evaluation a difficult task?

4. Delineate the various categories of national government policies giving examples of each.

Research Topics and Practical Applications

1. Choose a specific governmental program or policy on which you can readily find information in your school library. Examples might include a specific environmental law or regulation, a social welfare policy, a program promoting science or technology, or any examples you might find in your text. Research the policy and follow it through the stages in the policy process. How and why did the policy originally appear on the agenda? What strategy was chosen and why? By what means was the policy adopted? How was the policy implemented? Has the policy been formally evaluated? How would you evaluate the policy? You might wish to present your answer in an outline or diagram form.

2. The text explains that the issues on the policy agenda are always changing and gives examples of the dominate issues that were present in different decades. Using your understanding of American society and the issues we are presently facing, play the role of futurist and make a list of the issues that may be present on the policy agenda in the first few decades of the twenty-first century. Place a priority on the issues. Which do you believe the government will have to deal with first? What controversies might surround each of the issues? What policy options might you suggest to deal with the issues and what constraints will exist in finding a solution to the issues?

ANSWER KEY

Completion

1. policy
2. policy agenda
3. strategy
4. systems
5. Elitism
6. incrementalism
7. policy implementation
8. policy evaluation
9. bureaucratic model
10. Pluralism

True-False

1. F
2. T
3. T
4. F
5. F
6. F
7. T

Multiple Choice

1. c
2. b
3. c
4. c
5. c
6. d
7. a
8. c
9. a
10. d

Chapter 14

PUBLIC POLICY AND ECONOMICS

CHAPTER REVIEW

Learning Objectives

After studying Chapter 14 you should be able to:

1. Define laissez-faire and socialism.

2. Define protectionism and free trade.

3. Identify and define fiscal policy and monetary policy as well as the differences between the two.

4. Distinguish and define the major components of the national budget.

5. Define the terms deficit, debt, and surplus and be able to relate their relationship to the budget.

6. Comprehend and identify mandatory programs as well as their effect on the national budget.

7. Comprehend the budgeting process as well as the major players involved in the different stages of the process.

8. Identify several examples of attempts to control deficit spending.

Chapter Outline and Summary

I. Introduction

    A. Economic issues typically are high on the political agenda because they affect so many people.

B. Economic policy comprises the decisions that government makes that affect the production, distribution, and consumption of goods; the provision of services; the flow of income; and the distribution of wealth.

II. Government and Economic Policy

A. Basic Issues of Economic Policy

1. Should government involve itself in economic affairs at all?

a. Laissez-faire is French for "leave things alone." It is the belief that government should not interfere in the workings of the economy.

b. Socialism, on the other hand, is the belief that people will be best off if economic decision making is completely under the control of the government.

2. If government is involved, should its role be to stabilize the economy or should it remain neutral?

a. Before the New Deal and Great Depression, the belief was that the government should not interfere with the natural booms and busts of the economic cycle. The economy will correct itself.

b. Since then, the predominant view is that government should take an active role in stabilizing the economy.

c. The debate is further complicated with the presence of a global economy.

3. If government is to achieve stability, which policies achieve that goal?

a. Active involvement entails government adjusting such items as its spending or taxing decisions.

b. Passive involvement entails the government shaping general economic activity in an effort to entice individuals and private companies to stimulate the economy.

4. Should government promote or discourage particular types of economic activity?

a. Protectionism is the belief that government should protect American business and industry by restricting the flow of foreign goods into the United States.

b. Free trade, by contrast, is the belief that American interests are better served by allowing foreign producers to sell their goods without restriction. Businesses which cannot compete should die natural economic deaths.

B. Fiscal and Monetary Policy

1. Fiscal policy is governmental decisions about taxing and spending that affect the economic life of a nation.

a. Office of Management and Budget (OMB) is the Executive Office agency that provides the president with budgetary information.

b. The OMB compiles the president's annual budget proposal to Congress.

2. Monetary policy is government decisions about how much money should circulate

and what the cost of borrowing money, the interest rate, should be.

    a. *McCulloch v. Maryland*—In this Supreme Court case, the court made the decision that Congress had an "implied power" to charter a national bank, the Federal Reserve System.

    b. The Federal Reserve shapes the economy by manipulating the money supply and interest rates.

III. The Deficit and the National Budget

  A. The Deficit as a Political Issue

    1. Deficit is an excess of government expenditures over revenues.

    2. Debt is the sum of the deficits of prior years.

    3. Surplus is an excess of government revenues over government expenditures.

  B. Major Components of the National Budget

    1. National Defense

      a. A constitutional responsibility.

      b. Spending on defense consumes a significant portion of the budget.

      c. The breakup of the Soviet Union and the end of the Cold War ushered periods of decline in defense spending; however, this trend has reversed as the nation combats terrorism.

    2. Payments for Individuals

      a. A second major spending category in the budget.

      b. Includes social welfare programs

        (i) Social Security—monthly checks to retired and disabled citizens.

        (ii) Medicare—medical care for the elderly and disabled.

        (iii) unemployment compensation—weekly checks to short term unemployed.

        (iv) food stamps—food vouchers for the needy.

        (v) Medicaid—medical care for the needy.

        (vi) supplemental security income—supplemental cash for the needy.

      c. Relatively new programs started only within the past half-century.

    3. Interest Costs

      a. Net interest represent the charges that the government must pay to the public for the use of money borrowed.

      b. The amount of interest paid will vary with the interest rates and the time period of the loan.

4. All Other
   a. Includes programs such as cancer research, space exploration, highway construction, and environmental protection.
   b. Spending in this category fluctuates with the spending in the other categories.

C. Mandatory Programs in the Budget

1. Mandatory programs are government programs in which spending automatically increases without any action by the Congress (e.g., Social Security).
2. Social entitlements are programs whereby eligible individuals receive benefits according to law.
3. The concept of mandatory spending illustrates the obstacles Congress and the president face in their attempts to cut deficits.

IV. The President and Congress in the Budgeting Process

A. Introduction

1. Budgets are a planned statement of expenditure that includes specific categories of spending.
2. Budget makers cannot accurately predict the flow of dollars into and out of the federal treasury in a given year.
3. The budget making process is also highly decentralized as it is shaped by a large number of individuals and groups both inside and outside the government.

B. The Stages of Budgeting

1. Presidential proposal is a compilation of agency request for funds, shaped by presidential priorities and submitted to the Congress.
2. Congressional response is a review of the presidential proposals, and then molding them to fit into congressional priorities. If the president agrees, then they become law.
3. Agency expenditures of funds according to the budget laws enacted by Congress and signed by the president.
4. The fiscal year is a 12-month period starting October 1 and ending September 30 of the following calendar year.

C. The President in the Budget Process

1. The president is the single most powerful person in the budget-making process.
2. The president has the power to propose a budget. Although the budget may not be adopted as submitted, the president sets the tone for debate in the budget process.
3. The president also has the power to veto budget bills passed by the Congress.

D. Congress and Budgeting

1. Congressional power to make decisions on the budget are constitutionally bound.

2. Congress is made of 535 individuals representing different parts of the country and inevitably reflecting conflicting views.

3. Each branch of Congress has "money" committees along with all the other committees that influence the budget.

4. Congress must take two separate steps before money can actually be spent.

   a. Authorization is the congressional enactment that creates or continues a policy program and the agency administering it.

   b. Appropriation is the congressional enactment that funds an authorized program with a specific sum of money.

V. The Search for Better Budget Procedures

A. Introduction

1. Line-item veto is a proposed amendment to the Constitution that would give the president the power to accept some spending items in a bill but may also reject other spending items in the same bill.

2. Balanced budget amendment is a proposed amendment to the Constitution that would require the federal government to operate with a budget in which revenues equaled or exceeded expenditures.

3. The Congressional Budget and Impoundment Control Act of 1974 was an effort to view the budget process through a comprehensive system rather than piecemeal.

   a. Created budget committees.

   b. Established a budget decision timetable. Also allowed for "continuing resolutions" which allows spending at the previous years levels if Congress has not met the deadline.

   c. Changed the fiscal year start date from July 1 to October 1 to allow more time to review.

   d. Created the Congressional Budget Office (CBO), which provides Congress with budgetary expertise independent of the president's proposal and to clarify budgetary choices.

4. Gramm-Rudman-Hollings (Balanced Budget and Emergency Deficit Control Act of 1985)

    a. Mandated progressively higher annual cuts, sequestration, to achieve a balanced budget by 1991.

    b. The Supreme Court declared the procedure for automatic across-the-board cuts to be unconstitutional.

    c. Budget Enforcement Act of 1990 was an effort to reduce budget deficits by placing a focus on ceilings or caps on specific categories of spending.

VI. Summary

Key Terms, Concepts, and Personalities

After studying Chapter 14 you should be able to identify and describe the significance of:

appropriation

authorization

balanced budget amendment

budget

Budget Enforcement Act of 1990

Congressional Budget and Impoundment
    Control Act of 1974

Congressional Budget Office

continuing resolution

debt

deficit

depression

economic policy

fiscal policy

fiscal year

free trade

Gramm-Rudman-Hollings

laissez-faire

line-item veto

mandatory programs

monetary policy

net interest

Office of Management and Budget

protectionism

recession

sequestration

social entitlements

socialism

surplus

TESTING YOUR UNDERSTANDING

Completion

1. _____ _____ is French for "leave things alone." It is the belief that government should not interfere in the workings of the economy.

2. The belief that government should protect American business and industry by restricting the flow of foreign goods into the U.S. is called _____.

3. The _____ _____ _____ _____
_____ is the Executive Office agency that provides the president with budgetary information.

4. Monetary Policy is government decisions about how much _____ should circulate and what the interest rate should be.

5. _____ is the sum of the deficits of prior years.

6. Government programs in which spending automatically increases without any action by the Congress are called _____ _____.

7. The president has the power to _____ budget bills passed by the Congress.

8. _____ is the congressional enactment that funds an authorized program with a specific sum of money.

9. The _____ _____ amendment is a proposed amendment to the Constitution that would require the federal government to operate with a budget in which revenues equaled or exceeded expenditures.

10. The _____ _____ is the 12-month period beginning October 1 and ending September 30 the following calendar year.

Compare and Contrast

1. laissez-faire and socialism

2. protectionism and free trade

3. fiscal policy and monetary policy

4. deficit spending and surplus revenues

5. national defense, payments to individuals, and interest costs

6. mandatory programs and social entitlements

7. the president in the budgetary process and the Congress in the budgetary process

8. line-item veto and balanced budget amendment

True-False

1. Socialism is the belief that government should not interfere in the workings of the economy. T F

2. Free-trade is the belief that American interests are better served by allowing foreign producers to sell their goods without restriction. T F

3. Fiscal policy is governmental decisions about taxing and spending that affect the economic life of a nation. T F

4. Monetary policy is government decisions about how much money should circulate and what the interest rate should be. T F

5. The Federal Reserve shapes the economy by submitting a budget proposal to the Congress for approval. T F

6. Social Security, Medicare, and food stamps are all examples of payments for individuals. T F

7. Incrementalism is a model of decision making that holds that new policies differ substantially from existing policies. T F

8. Line-item veto would give the president the power to accept some spending items in a bill and reject other items in the same bill. T F

9. Congress can either use authorization or appropriation in allowing funds to be spent. T F

10. Gramm-Rudman-Hollings mandated sequestration to achieve a balanced budget by 1991. T F

Multiple Choice

1. Laissez-faire is the belief that:
   a. government should take an active role in stabilizing the economy.
   b. government should take complete control in economic decisions.
   c. government should not interfere in the workings of the economy.
   d. government should interfere in foreign as well as domestic economies.

2. Government involvement in the economy has increased dramatically since the:
   a. line-item veto was first utilized by President Clinton.
   b. establishment of the Congressional Budget Office (CBO).
   c. ratification of the Gramm-Rudman-Hollings Act.
   d. New Deal and Great Depression.

3. Protectionism is the belief that the government should protect:
   a. American business and industry by restricting the flow of foreign goods into the U.S.
   b. all economic decision making by placing the decisions completely under the control of the government.
   c. American business and industry by manipulating the money supply and interest rates.
   d. the economic decision making by manipulating the information presented to the Congress and nation.

4. The fiscal policy of the government entails:
   a. the submission of governmental budgets on a 12-month time frame starting with October 1 and ending with September 30 of every year.
   b. manipulating the money supply and interest rate.
   c. decisions about taxing and spending that affect the economic life of a nation.
   d. excesses in government revenues over government expenditures.

5. Monetary policy is government decisions about:
   a. how much money should circulate and what the interest rate should be.
   b. taxing and spending that affect the economic life of a nation.
   c. allowing foreign producers to sell their goods without restriction.
   d. enticing individuals and private companies to stimulate the economy.

6. Deficit is an excess of government:
   a. revenues over expenditures.
   b. expenditures on national defense.
   c. expenditures on Social Security.
   d. expenditures over revenues.

7. The following are all examples of major components of the national budget *except*:
   a. national defense.
   b. economic development.
   c. interest costs.
   d. payments for individuals.

8. Mandatory programs are government programs in which:
   a. individual state participation is mandated by federal law.
   b. spending is restricted to only programs mandated by federal law.
   c. spending automatically increases without any action by the Congress.
   d. spending is restricted to congressionally mandated programs.

9. The single most important person in the budget-making process is the:
   a. chairman of the Federal Reserve.
   b. president of the United States.
   c. chairman of the Congressional Budget Office.
   d. Chief Justice of the United States.

10. The following are all examples of attempts to control the national debt *except*:
    a. balanced budget amendment.
    b. socialism.
    c. line-item veto.
    d. Gramm-Rudman-Hollings.

Essay

1. Explain the various major components of the national budget and elaborate on the interaction the various components have on one another.

2. Identify a specific example of a mandatory program in the budget and expand on how it and incrementalism create an obstacle for the president and Congress in their attempt to cut deficits.

3. What was the significance of *McCulloch* v. *Maryland?* Discuss how this Supreme Court case is still influencing the American economy today.

4. Identify the major components of fiscal and monetary policy. Differentiate between the two and identify how both are used by the government today.

5. Identify three examples of current attempts by the government to control deficit spending. Characterize their major components as well as the success and failures of the individual attempts.

Research Topics and Practical Applications

1. Find copies of a local government's budget proposal as well as the approved budget for several budget cycles. Answer the following questions for the budgets you chose:
   a. How was the final approved budget changed from the original proposal?
   b. Who were the individuals involved in submitting, adapting and approving the budget?
   c. Were there signs of incrementalism?
   d. What are specific examples of social entitlement programs, what percentage of the budget did they encompass, and were there changes in priorities from one year to the next?
   e. Are there any examples of self-imposed restrictions regarding the local government's budget?

2. Follow the federal budget cycle. What are the major components of the president's budget proposal? How do they differ from the previous year and were they affected by national and international events? What were the congressional responses to the proposed budget and were there any examples of personal congressional influence or adaptations to the budget? Did the president accept all the changes with little or no debate or was there an intense debate?

ANSWER KEY

Completion

1. Laissez-faire
2. protectionism
3. Office of Management and Budget
4. money
5. Debt
6. mandatory programs
7. veto
8. Appropriation
9. balanced budget
10. fiscal year

True-False

1. F
2. T
3. T
4. T
5. F
6. T
7. F
8. T
9. F
10. T

Multiple Choice

1. c
2. d
3. a
4. c
5. a
6. d
7. b
8. c
9. b
10. b

Chapter 15

DOMESTIC POLICY

CHAPTER REVIEW

Learning Objectives

After studying Chapter 15 you should be able to:

1. Define domestic policy and identify several examples of domestic policy programs which have been designed to meet specific needs.

2. Understand the evolution of the domestic policy issues and programs as well as be able to identify shifts in the policies and the causes of those shifts.

3. List the major milestones in the transition from a national government with little involvement in individual needs to a national government that is well ingrained in individual domestic issues.

4. Identify major policies and programs designed to alleviate the suffering of the aged, poor, disabled, or unemployed and list the major components of each.

5. Define and understand the criticisms of major programs as well as identify some attempts to correct the problems listed.

6. Understand the reason for the Environmental Protection Agency, the reason it has reached a prevalent status in current society, and some of the major regulations and restrictions it has established.

Chapter Outline and Summary

I. Debates Over Public Purposes

    A. Introduction

        1. Domestic policy is a public policy that is comprised of policy decisions on matters affecting individuals within a political system.

a. Domestic policy is affected by the self-interest of various groups and individuals.

b. Self-interest is frequently cloaked in the mantle of *the national interest*.

B. Social Welfare Policies

1. Social welfare are governmental programs directed specifically toward promoting the well-being of individuals and families (e.g., social insurance).

2. Social entitlements are programs whereby eligible individuals receive benefits according to law (e.g., Social Security).

II. The Development of Federal Social Welfare Policy

A. Introduction

1. The domestic activities of the national government before the Twentieth century were very limited.

B. The Philosophy of Social Darwinism

1. Social Darwinism is a set of ideas applying Charles Darwin's theory of biological evolution to society and holding that societal relationships occur within a struggle for survival in which only the fittest survive.

a. The theory offered intellectual justification for limited government and unfettered growth of industry.

b. Government should not assume the role of providing for social welfare because such action would interfere with the natural forces acting to improve society as a whole.

C. The Progressive Era

1. The Progressive Era was an urban reform movement that called for direct primaries, restriction on corporations, and improved public services. It replaced the corrupt politics with the civil service system.

D. The New Deal Policy Revolution

1. The New Deal encompassed the policy initiatives enacted during the first two terms of President Franklin D. Roosevelt in an effort to relieve suffering of those touched by the Great Depression.

a. Revolutionary policy initiatives (e.g., FDIC, Social Security, and unemployment compensation).

b. Established a pervasive and active role for the national government. Public expectations that the government "do something" about social and economic problems arose from the Roosevelt presidency.

E. Expansion of the National Role in the Great Society

　　1. The Great Society included policy initiatives enacted during President Lyndon Johnson's terms. It called for aggressive government action to help the poor and disadvantaged.

　　　　a. The Civil Rights Act of 1964 and the Voting Rights Act of 1965 finally provided by law the rights long denied to African Americans.

　　　　b. The Equal Opportunity Act and the Food Stamp Act of 1964 explicitly dealt with the plight of the poor.

　　　　c. The Elementary and Secondary Education Act of 1964 provided federal aid for the disadvantaged in the country's schools.

　　　　d. Perhaps the most important was the Social Security Act amendment in 1965 provided health care for the aged (Medicare) and the poor (Medicaid).

III. The National Government as Social Insurer

　A. Introduction

　　1. Social insurance programs are programs that provide cash or services to the aged, disabled, and the unemployed, regardless of income level.

　B. Social Security

　　1. Social Security Act of 1935 was landmark legislation that firmly established for the first time a social welfare role for the national government by providing old age insurance, unemployment compensation, and grants to the states to provide cash assistance to dependent children and to the blind, disabled and aged.

　　　　a. In terms of expenditures, numbers of people, and intensity of political support, Social Security is the national government's largest and single most important domestic policy.

　　　　b. By the late 1970s and early 1980s it had become clear that with a declining birth rate and longer life expectancies the expenditures would soon exceed revenues. As a result, the future of Social Security has been an almost constant topic on the American political scene.

　C. Medicare

　　1. Medicare is a public health insurance program in which government pays the providers of health care for medical services given to patients who are aged or disabled. Medicare is a program with two parts:

　　　　a. Hospital Insurance (HI), funded by a portion of the Social Security tax paid into a hospital trust fund. After a patient pays a deductible, Medicare covers hospital costs for two months, with patients sharing costs after that period.

b. Supplemental Medical Insurance (SMI) is a program that, after a patient pays a deductible amount, funds physician and outpatient services. SMI is voluntary and is funded by premiums paid by enrollees and general revenues from the federal treasury.

D. Unemployment Compensation

1. Unemployment compensation is a social insurance policy that grants temporary financial assistance to the unemployed. It is not designed for the chronically unemployed but for those who need financial assistance to keep afloat between jobs.

IV. Public Policy and Economic Inequality

A. Introduction

1. Means-tested programs are a type of social welfare programs in which government provides cash or in-kind benefits to individuals who qualify by having little or no income.

B. Measures of Economic Inequality

1. Quintiles consist of dividing the families into five groups according to the proportion of total money each group receives.
    a. Perfect income equality would mean that each fifth of the population of families receives 20 percent of all the money income—that each quintile receives an equal slice of the money pie.
    b. However, great income inequality persists as the lowest group receives about 3.5 percent of the money pie while the highest group receives over 50 percent of the money pie.

2. Another measure of economic inequality is the proportion of the total population classified as poor in the United States.
    a. The term poverty is a human construct and does not have the same meaning in all societies.
    b. Relative deprivation is a definition of poverty that holds that individuals with less, regardless of their absolute income level, will feel poor or deprived relative to those who have more.
    c. Poverty threshold is an income level, different by family size and adjusted annually for inflation, below which individuals are defined as being poor.

C. Poverty as a Political and Social Problem

1. Social scientists have generally offered two sets of explanations for why people are poor.
   a. The first holds that people are poor because they lack *personal qualities,* such as ambition or intelligence.
   b. The second explanation centers on the kind of social, economic, and cultural *environment* that is likely to be fertile ground for poverty.

2. Working poor are individuals who, despite being employed or seeking employment, are still defined as poor because their low earnings are not enough to put them above the poverty threshold.

3. Underclass is defined as a proportion of the poor comprised of individuals isolated from the rest of society and for whom poverty is a continuing way of life.

4. Curative strategies are policy strategies designed to reach the fundamental causes of poverty and to enable individuals to get out of poverty and lead productive, self-sufficient lives.

5. Alleviative strategies are policy strategies designed to make poverty more bearable for individuals rather than designed to attack poverty by reaching its fundamental causes.
   a. Aid to Families with Dependent Children (AFDC) is one of the oldest alleviate strategies that provides cash assistance to needy children and an adult relative and, in participating states, an unemployed parent.
   b. These strategies, welfare programs, were among the most controversial poverty programs because of the perception that it creates a "welfare dependency" that is passed from one generation of families to the next, with little hope of breaking out of the vicious cycle.
   c. Welfare Reform Act of 1996
      (i) Changed the name from Aid to Families with Dependent Children (AFDC) to Temporary Assistance for Needy Families (TANF) to emphasize the temporary nature of the program.

D. Temporary Assistance for Needy Families

1. It placed a two-year limit on the receipt of benefits.
2. Required recipients to work at least part time while receiving benefits.
3. Provided some exemptions for education and job training.

E.   Supplemental Security Income

    1.   Supplemental Security Income (SSI) is a social welfare program administered by the Social Security Administration whereby the national government guarantees a certain level of income for the needy, aged, blind, and disabled.

F.   Medicaid

    1.   Medicaid is a means-tested medical care program providing in-kind medical benefits for the poor.

G.   The Food Stamp Program

    1.   Food Stamp Program is a means-tested program that provides the eligible needy with monetary assistance that can be used to purchase food.

V.   Environmental Policy

A.   Introduction

    1.   Environmental protection is a domestic policy designed to regulate various types of pollution.

B.   The Evolution of Environmental Policy

    1.   An environmental consciousness was slow to develop in the U.S.

    2.   The struggle was between conservationists and preservationists.

    3.   It was not until the latter half of the 20th Century that an environmental consciousness developed in the U.S.

    4.   The 1980s and 1990s witnessed a shift from a national environmental focus to a global focus (e.g., global warming, ozone depletion).

C.   The Actors and their Roles

    1.   The president is a major actor and sets the tone with appointments and policies advocated.

    2.   Congress passes the environmental legislation (e.g., Clean Air Act).

    3.   The bureaucracy implements the policy.

       a.   The Interior Department (e.g., BLM and National Park Service) and Agriculture Department (e.g., Forestry Service) have a role in environmental policy.

    4.   The courts are active in environmental policy issues due mainly to the litigation associated with the Endangered Species Act and the requirement for environmental impact statements.

5. Interest groups can be broken down into two main categories
   a. Environmental and citizen activist groups.
   b. Business groups and supporters.
6. The media calls attention to environmental issues through their gatekeeper role.

D. Environmentalism on the Policy Agenda

   1. Quality of life issues and health concerns are closely tied to the environment.
   2. The principle of scientific uncertainty complicates environmental policy.
   3. Global issues like global warming and ozone depletion are now on the environmental agenda.
   4. Risk assessment v. risk management.
      a. Risk assessment is the process of estimating the potentially dangerous consequences of damage that might be caused by a particular activity.
      b. Risk management is the process of making decisions that try to reduce or contain identified risks.

E. The Future of Environmental Policy

   1. Environmental policy challenges abound. When the environment and the economy come into conflict, which should take precedence?

VI. Summary

Key Terms, Concepts, and Personalities

After studying Chapter 15 you should be able to identify and describe the significance of:

alleviative strategies
curative strategies
domestic policy
Endangered Species Act
environmental impact statement
Environmental Protection Agency
food stamp program
Great Society
greenhouse effect
means-tested programs
Medicaid
social insurance programs

Medicare
National Priorities List
New Deal
poverty threshold
principle of scientific uncertainty
Progressive Era
relative deprivation
risk assessment
risk management
social Darwinism
social entitlements
Temporary Assistance for Needy Families

Social Security Act of 1935
social welfare
Super Fund
Supplemental Security Income

underclass
unemployment compensation
Welfare Reform Act
working poor

TESTING YOUR UNDERSTANDING

Completion

1. _____ _____ are governmental programs directed specifically toward promoting the well-being of individuals and families (e.g., social insurance).

2. The set of ideas that applied the theory of biological evolution to society and holding that societal relationships occur within a struggle for survival in which only the fittest survive is known as _____ _____.

3. The _____ _____ encompassed the policy initiatives enacted during President Lyndon Johnson's terms. It called for aggressive government action to help the poor and disadvantaged.

4. _____ is a public health insurance program in which government pays the providers of health care for medical services given to patients who are aged or disabled.

5. The idea that holds that individuals with less, regardless of their absolute income level, will feel poor or deprived relative to those who have more is called _____ _____.

6. _____ _____ are policy strategies designed to make poverty more bearable for individuals rather than designed to attack poverty by reaching its fundamental causes.

7. The _____ _____ _____ is a means-tested program that provides the eligible needy with monetary assistance to purchase food.

8. The independent agency that controls and abates air and water pollution and protects the environment from pollution from pollutants such as pesticides, radiation, and toxic substances is the _____ _____

_____.

9. The problem of _____ _____ complicates environmental policy.

10. _____ _____ is the process of estimating the potentially dangerous consequences of damage that might be caused by a particular activity.

Compare and Contrast

1. Social Darwinism and the Progressive Era

2. New Deal and Great Society

3. Medicare and Medicaid

4. working poor and underclass

5. curative strategies and alleviative strategies

6. risk assessment and risk management

True-False

1. Social entitlements are programs whereby eligible individuals receive benefits according to law. T F

2. The Progressive Era was a time when applying Charles Darwin's theory of biological evolution to society and holding that societal relationships occur within a struggle for survival in which only the fittest survive. T F

3. The New Deal encompassed the policy initiatives enacted during President Lyndon Johnson's terms. T F

4. The Great Society policy initiatives were enacted during the first two terms of President Franklin D. Roosevelt in an effort to relieve suffering of those touched by the Depression. T F

5. Social insurance programs are welfare programs that provide cash or services to the aged, disabled, and the unemployed, regardless of income level. T F

6. Medicare is a public health insurance program in which government pays the providers of health care for medical services given to patients who are aged or disabled. T F

7. Working poor are individuals who, despite being employed or seeking employment, are still defined as poor because their low earnings are not enough to put them above the poverty threshold. T F

8. The Welfare Reform Act abolished the requirement that welfare recipients work at least part time in order to receive benefits. T F

9. Medicaid is a means-tested medical care program providing in-kind medical benefits for the poor. T F

10. Risk assessment is the process of making decisions that try to reduce or contain identified risks. T F

Multiple Choice

1. Social entitlements are programs whereby eligible individuals receive benefits according to:
   a. age.
   b. law.
   c. social status.
   d. presidential priorities.

2. All of the following are programs initiated during the Great Society initiatives *except*:
   a. Civil Rights Act of 1964.
   b. Elementary and Secondary Act.
   c. Social Security.
   d. Food Stamp Act.

3. Social insurance programs are welfare programs that provide cash or services to the aged, disabled, and the unemployed:
   a. regardless of income level.
   b. based on income level.
   c. regardless of national debt.
   d. based on work history.

4. The public health insurance program in which government pays the providers of health care for medical services given to patients who are aged or disabled is known as:
   a. Medicaid.
   b. Supplemental Medical Insurance.
   c. Social Security.
   d. Medicare.

5. The social insurance policy that grants temporary financial assistance to the unemployed is known as:
   a. Social Security.
   b. Supplemental Medical Insurance.
   c. unemployment compensation.
   d. relative deprivation.

6. Means-tested programs are a type of social welfare program in which government provides cash or in-kind benefits to individuals who qualify by having:
   a. little or no income.
   b. worked a minimum of 10 years.
   c. invested a set amount.
   d. lived long lives.

7. Individuals who, despite being employed or seeking employment, are still defined as poor because their low earnings are not enough to put them above the poverty threshold are known as:
   a. underclass.
   b. social scientists.
   c. incrementalists.
   d. working poor.

8. All of the following are attempts at welfare reform *except*:
   a. two year limits on receiving benefits.
   b. unemployment compensation.
   c. changing the title from AFDC to TANF.
   d. requiring recipients to work at least part time.

9. All of the following are examples of public policies to address economic inequality *except*:
   a. Supplemental Security Income.
   b. Medicaid.
   c. Social Darwinism.
   d. Food Stamp Program.

10. The process of making decisions that try to reduce or contain identified risks is called:
    a. risk assessment.
    b. curative strategies.
    c. alleviative strategies.
    d. risk management.

11. A book written by Rachel Carson in 1962 that chronicled the impact of DDT on song bird populations was called:
    a. *Limits to Growth*.
    b. *The Population Bomb*.
    c. *Silent Spring*.
    d. none of the above

12. The _____ received considerable attention as it attempted to address global issues such as ozone depletion and global warming.
    a. 1992 Earth Summit
    b. 1997 Kyoto Protocol
    c. 2000 China Summit
    d. Brazil Forum

13. The _____ focused attention on the relationship between the greenhouse gas carbon dioxide and global warming by mandating carbon dioxide reductions to pre-1990 levels for industrialized countries.
    a. 1992 Earth Summit
    b. 1997 Kyoto Protocol
    c. 2000 China Summit
    d. Brazil Forum

14. The _____ is a significant environmental bureaucratic actor since it oversees the BLM and National Park Service.
    a. Environmental Protection Agency
    b. Interior Department
    c. Agriculture Department
    d. White House

15. A(n) _____ requires a study be undertaken to determine the impact of a proposed project on the environment whenever federal funds are being used.
    a. environmental impact statement
    b. assessment report
    c. risk assessment report
    d. risk management report

16. The _____ was legislation in 1980 to identify and clean up the worst hazardous waste sites throughout the United States.
    a. Greenhouse Effect Act
    b. Priorities Act
    c. Super Fund
    d. Ozone Depletion Act

17. A good example of the media's gatekeeper role affecting environmental policy is the:
    a. Super Fund.
    b. national priorities list.
    c. Endangered Species Act.
    d. Love Canal incident.

18. The _____ theory states that gasses such as carbon dioxide are responsible for global warming.
    a. greenhouse effect
    b. national priorities list
    c. Super Fund
    d. ozone depletion

19. The principle of _____ complicates environmental policy since it makes it difficult to say with absolute certainty that there is a cause-effect relationship (e.g., greenhouse gasses causing global warming).
    a. scientific uncertainty
    b. risk assessment
    c. risk management
    d. none of the above

20. The process of estimating dangerous consequences of damage that might be caused by a particular practice is called:
   a. scientific uncertainty.
   b. risk assessment.
   c. risk management.
   d. none of the above

Essay

1. Explain the concept of Social Darwinism and relate the concept to the biological and scientific base on which it was based.

2. What events ushered in the now prevalent concept of government involvement in domestic issues? Explain the various milestones in the social welfare programs and define how those ideas and policies are still affecting society today.

3. Define the major components of the Social Security Act of 1935 and how they relate to the issues of national budgets, political debate, and individual concerns.

4. What is the significance of the Environmental Protection Agency and how do its regulations affect life in the United States today?

Research Topics and Practical Applications

1. Research the last three presidencies. Were there any major changes in the domestic policy and its concentration on social welfare programs? Was political party identification an indicator of preferences and spending requests? Was the geographical or demographic background of the president an influence on the social welfare policy initiatives? Were social welfare programs completely independent of the presidency and functioned without their influence?

2. Identify a specific regulation of the Environmental Protection Agency. What is the law and what are its major functions and requirements? Are there any other levels of government which are affected, influenced or mandated by the EPA's regulation? How does the regulation affect the private, for profit sector? How are individual citizens affected by the regulation? Is the economy of either the nation, state, private sector, or individual affected substantially by the regulation?

ANSWER KEY

Completion

1. Social welfare
2. Social Darwinism
3. Great Society
4. Medicare
5. relative deprivation
6. Alleviative strategies
7. Food Stamp Program
8. Environmental Protection Agency
9. scientific uncertainty
10. Risk assessment

True-False

1. T
2. F
3. F
4. F
5. T
6. T
7. T
8. F
9. T
10. F

Multiple Choice

1. b
2. c
3. a
4. d
5. c
6. a
7. d
8. b
9. c
10. d
11. c
12. a
13. b
14. b
15. a
16. c
17. d
18. a
19. a
20. b

Chapter 16

FOREIGN POLICY

CHAPTER REVIEW

Learning Objectives

After studying Chapter 16 you should be able to:

1. Explain the role of America in the world, specifically focusing on isolationism, internationalism, the cold war, and the post–cold war.

2. Discuss the policy machinery of foreign policy.

3. Define the Department of State.

4. Define the Central Intelligence Agency.

5. Define the Department of Defense.

6. Discuss how public moods and general attitudes affect domestic policy and national security.

7. Discuss current issues in foreign and defense policy.

Chapter Outline and Summary

I. The International System

    A. Introduction

        1. The international system is complex with a multitude of actors, which complicates foreign policy making.

B. Major Actors in the International System

   1. The Sovereign State

      a. The sovereign state has been the major actor for the past 300 years.

         (i) A state is defined as an entity that has defined borders, a sovereign government and a population of citizens (e.g., the United States).

         (ii) Sovereignty is an important concept associated with the state.

         (iii) National interest is a difficult term to define since it is what is perceived to be in the best interests of the state.

   2. International Governmental Organization (IGO)

      a. IGOs are defined as an entity that has a headquarters staff, and two or more states have joined (e.g., United Nations).

   3. Non Governmental Organization (NGO)

      a. NGOs are defined as a non-state entity that conducts business across borders (e.g., Wal-Mart).

C. Structure of the International System

   1. The structure of the international system helps to define foreign policy.

      a. Polarity (poles of power) determines the power structure of the international system.

      b. Cleavages (splits) in the international system such as the North-South cleavage, which is determined by the standard of living difference between the developed countries of the northern hemisphere and the developing countries of the southern hemisphere, influence the international system.

II. America's Role in the World

   A. Introduction

      1. Isolationism—a belief that America should not involve itself in the quarrels of Europe and Asia and should pursue a policy of military nonintervention.

         a. Dominated American thought in the 1920s and 1930s.

         b. After WWI, America withdrew from world affairs.

      2. Internationalism—a foreign policy perspective that concludes that America's interests in peace abroad and liberty at home requires its permanent involvement in world affairs.

         a. Occurred after WWII.

         b. America took the lead to form the United Nations in 1945.

   B. The Cold War and Post-Cold War Era

      1. Problems began during WWII.

a. America worked closely with Great Britain and left the Soviet Union out during the atomic bomb project.

b. President Truman curtailed military supplies to the Soviets.

c. The Soviets contended that they were never treated as a genuine ally by the United States.

2. Ideological differences between the democratic West and the communist East added to the lack of trust.

3. The lack of free elections in Eastern Europe was resented by the West.

4. Truman Doctrine—a policy, proclaimed by President Harry Truman in 1947, in which the United States would oppose the expansion of communism anywhere in the world.

5. Marshall Plan—an American program begun after WWII for the economic rehabilitation of Western Europe.

6. The Soviet Union responded to these two endeavors by tightening their control over Eastern Europe.

7. The cold war did see real military conflict.

a. Korean conflict (1950–1953)—the American military was deployed to the Korean peninsula when communist forces crossed into South Korea.

b. Vietnam conflict (1961–1973)—a decade of heavy fighting with a U.S. loss of over 50,000 lives.

c. These conflicts contributed to new approaches dealing with communism known as détente and the Nixon Doctrine.

d. Détente—a French word meaning "relaxation" that was applied to American-Soviet relations in the early 1970s.

e. Nixon Doctrine—a policy proclaimed by President Nixon in 1969 stipulating that the United States will support its allies with economic and military aid but that the allies should provide the bulk of the manpower for their own defense.

8. The cold war came to an end with two events:

a. By the end of 1989, all of the governments of the Soviet Union's Eastern European allies had collapsed.

b. Germany was united in the summer of 1990.

9. America is redefining its role to accommodate the changing international sphere.

III. The Policy Machinery

    A. The President

        1. The president derives foreign policy constitutional authority in Article II, Section 2, of the Constitution.

            a. Commander-in-Chief of the armed forces.

            b. Make treaties.

            c. Make appointments (ambassadors)

        2. Presidential pronouncements (e.g., Monroe Doctrine, Nixon Doctrine, Carter Doctrine, Bush Doctrine) set the tone for U.S. foreign policy.

    B. The Bureaucracy

        1. Department of State is responsible for the routine daily functions of foreign policy, it represents the U.S. abroad, is involved in international negotiations, supervises foreign aid programs, promotes cultural and educational exchange, and makes policy recommendations to the president.

            a. Heading the department is the secretary of state, who reports directly to the president.

            b. Beneath the secretary is the deputy secretary of state, six undersecretaries, and a counselor.

            c. Below that level is a number of bureaus that monitor events around the world.

            d. Attached to the State Department are three additional organizations.

                (i) U.S. Permanent Representative to the United Nations—represents the United States in the UN.

                (ii) U.S. Agency for International Development—coordinates economic assistance programs.

                (iii) Office of International Information Programs—directs overseas information programs.

        2. The Central Intelligence Agency was established by the 1947 National Security Act and is responsible for gathering information and coordinating foreign intelligence operations in the federal government.

            a. During the cold war, the CIA conducted secret political activities.

            b. Aided in the installment of pro-American governments in Iran and Guatemala.

            c. Presidents Ford and Carter set firm limits on CIA operations by placing covert activities under close presidential control.

            d. The dilemma of the CIA is the question of the agency's covert nature in a democratic society.

3. The Department of Defense was established by the 1947 National Security Act and is responsible for formulating military policy and maintaining the armed forces.

    a. Comprised of three basic organizations: the Office of the Secretary of Defense, the Joints Chiefs of Staff and the separate armed services.

    b. Heading the department is the secretary of defense.

    c. Joints Chiefs of Staff—heads of the various armed services and their chair who advise the president and the secretary of defense on important military matters.

4. The National Security Advisor (NSA) is the "honest broker" advisor to the president since the NSA does not head a large bureaucracy.

C. The Role of Congress

1. Congress derives its foreign policy constitutional authority from Article I, Section 8, of the Constitution.

2. Congress plays a limited role of telling the president what the executive branch cannot do.

    a. Congress can limit the president's authority to conduct arms sales.

    b. Congress cannot do more in the area of foreign policy for three reasons: parochialism, organizational weakness, and lack of information.

D. Interest Groups/Public Opinion

1. Israeli lobby continues to lobby decision makers to support Israel.

2. The Cuban-American community has been able to affect U.S.-Cuban policy.

E. The Media

1. The "CNN Effect" can affect foreign policy public opinion by focusing attention on certain foreign policy issues.

IV. Summary

Key Terms, Concepts, and Personalities

After studying Chapter 16, you should be able to identify and describe the significance of:

Central Intelligence Agency
Containment
Department of Defense
Department of State
Détente

developed world
developing world
international governmental organization
    (IGO)
internationalism

Isolationism

Joint Chiefs of Staff

Marshall Plan

nation

national interest

national security advisor

nationalism

Nixon Doctrine

non-governmental organization (NGO)

North-South cleavage

Office of the Secretary of Defense

polarity

secretary of state

sovereignty

state (country)

Truman Doctrine

TESTING YOUR UNDERSTANDING

Completion

1. A(n) _____ is a group of people who share a common racial/ethnic background, language, religion, culture and customs.

2. _____ is the ability of a state to be able to control its own affairs.

3. A(n) _____ is a non-state entity that conducts business across borders.

4. _____ was the chief foreign policy goal of the U.S. during the cold war.

5. The _____ _____ _____ is considered the chief foreign policy advisor to the president.

6. Public moods, or general attitudes, are important because they can place limits on the choices available to _____ _____.

7. Public support never wavered during the _____ _____ in 1991.

8. According to the 1973 War Powers Act, congressional approval is needed for the president to send troops into combat for more than _____ days.

9. Congress can limit the president's authority to conduct _____ _____.

10. The Department of _____ was established by the National Security Act in 1947.

Compare and Contrast

1. state, IGOs, and NGOs

2. developed world and developing world

3. isolationism and internationalism

4. Department of Defense, Department of State, and the Central Intelligence Agency

5. the three organizations of the Department of State

6. cold war and post–cold war

True-False

1. Internationalism dominated American thought in the 1920s and 1930s. T   F

2. Isolationism is a foreign policy that concludes liberty at home requires its permanent involvement in world affairs. T   F

3. State and nation mean basically the same thing. T   F

4. National interest is easy to define and is unchanging over time. T   F

5. A bi-polar structure dominated the international system during the cold war. T   F

6. The North-South cleavage refers to the economic development differences between industrialized countries in the northern hemisphere and poor countries in the southern hemisphere. T   F

7. The Truman Doctrine was a multi-billion dollar American aid plan to Europe.   T   F

8. The Office of the Secretary of Defense was created to ensure civilian control of the U.S. military. T   F

9. The Department of Defense was established in 1947 and is responsible for formulating military policy and maintaining the armed forces. T F

10. The national security advisor (NSA) is considered to be the "honest broker" advisor to the president since he/she is not influenced by a large bureaucracy like State or Defense.
    T F

Multiple Choice

1. A(n) _____ is defined as an entity that has defined borders, a sovereign government and a population of citizens.
    a. state
    b. nation
    c. IGO
    d. NGO

2. _____ is a difficult term to define and can change quickly with a change of leadership.
    a. State
    b. Nation
    c. Sovereignty
    d. National interest

3. A(n) _____ is defined as an entity that has a headquarters and staff, and two or more states have joined.
    a. state
    b. nation
    c. IGO
    d. NGO

4. A(n) _____ world is a more complicated international system since a variety of actors have power within the international arena.
    a. uni-polar
    b. bi-polar
    c. multi-polar
    d. none of the above

5. The _____ involves the economic development differences between the industrialized countries in the northern hemisphere and the developing countries in the southern hemisphere.
    a. N-S cleavage
    b. developed world
    c. developing world
    d. none of the above

6. The cold war saw military conflict in the form of the:
    a. Asian Conflict.
    b. Iraq Conflict.
    c. Japan Conflict.
    d. Korean Conflict.

7. A French word meaning "relaxation" that was applied to American-Soviet relations is:
    a. détente.
    b. louvif.
    c. fretege.
    d. volue.

8. The policy proclaimed in 1969 stipulating that the U.S. will support its allies with economic and military aid, but that the host country will be responsible for providing manpower for its own defense, is the:
    a. Truman Doctrine.
    b. Nixon Doctrine.
    c. Ford Doctrine.
    d. Kennedy Doctrine.

9. One of the events that ended the cold war was the unification of:
    a. Poland.
    b. Germany.
    c. Russia.
    d. Spain.

10. The secretary of state reports directly to the:
    a. president.
    b. Department of State.
    c. Congress.
    d. CIA.

11. Right below the secretary of state is the:
    a. undersecretary.
    b. coordinator.
    c. bureaus.
    d. deputy secretary of state.

12. Bureaus monitor events that are:
    a. in America.
    b. in Europe.
    c. around the world.
    d. in Asia.

13. This organization coordinates economic assistance programs:
    a. Office of International Information Programs.
    b. Agency for International Development.
    c. World Bank.
    d. Secretary of Economics.

14. This organization directs overseas information programs:
    a. Office of International Information Programs.
    b. Agency for International Development
    c. World Bank.
    d. Secretary of Economics.

15. The CIA aided in the installment of a pro-American government in:
    a. Iraq.
    b. Hungary.
    c. Turkey.
    d. Iran.

16. The _____ can set declaratory policy (foreign affairs) with pronouncements such as the Monroe and Truman Doctrines.
    a. president
    b. bureaucracy
    c. courts
    d. interest groups

17. The _____ is considered to be the chief military policy advisor to the president.
    a. president
    b. secretary of state
    c. secretary of defense
    d. chairman, JCS

Essay

1. Discuss how public moods influence foreign policy. Specifically, use the Vietnam Conflict and Gulf War. In the public's eye, what were the differences between these conflicts?

2. Explain the foreign policy machinery using the Department of State, Central Intelligence Agency, Department of Defense, and Congress.

3. Describe the foreign policy views of isolationism and internationalism. How did each one originate? Discuss the differences between the two views.

4. Discuss current issues in foreign and defense policy concentrating on economics of the world and how America has changed since 9/11.

Research Topics and Practical Application

1. Think back to 9/11. Where were you and what were you doing? Since that day has your view changed on foreign policy? If so, in what way? Use the theories of isolationism and internationalism to debate the new idea of preemptive strikes.

2. Research the beginnings of WWI, WWII, and the Vietnam Conflict. How did these wars begin? Discuss why America became involved in these conflicts and determine if each involvement was the result of isolationism or internationalism.

ANSWER KEY

Completion

1. nation
2. Sovereignty
3. NGO
4. Containment
5. secretary of state
6. policy makers
7. Gulf War
8. 60
9. arms control
10. Defense

True-False

1. F
2. F
3. F
4. F
5. T
6. T
7. F
8. T
9. T
10. T

Multiple Choice

1. a
2. d
3. c
4. c
5. a
6. d
7. a
8. b
9. b
10. a
11. d
12. c
13. b
14. a
15. d
16. a
17. d

CPSIA information can be obtained at www.ICGtesting.com
Printed in the USA
BVOW09s0334130814

362650BV00006B/16/P